Your Towns and Cities in the

Lincoln

in the Great War

Your Towns and Cities in the Great War

Lincoln
in the Great War

by Louise Blackah

Pen & Sword
MILITARY

First published in Great Britain in 2016 by
PEN & SWORD MILITARY
An imprint of
Pen & Sword Books Ltd
47 Church Street
Barnsley
South Yorkshire, S70 2AS

ISBN 978 1 78383 1 562

A CIP catalogue record for this book is
available from the British Library.

Printed and bound in England by
CPI Group (UK) Ltd, Croydon, CR0 4YY

Pen & Sword Books Ltd incorporates the imprints of Aviation, Atlas,
Family History, Fiction, Maritime, Military, Discovery, Politics,
History, Archaeology, Select, Wharncliffe Local History, Wharncliffe
True Crime, Military Classics, Wharncliffe Transport, Leo Cooper,
The Praetorian Press, Remember When, Seaforth Publishing and
Frontline Publishing.

For a complete list of Pen & Sword titles please contact
PEN & SWORD BOOKS LIMITED
47 Church Street, Barnsley, South Yorkshire, S70 2AS, England
E-mail: enquiries@pen-and-sword.co.uk
Website: www.pen-and-sword.co.uk

Contents

Acknowledgements   7

Introduction   9

1. 1914 – Eager for a Fight   11

2. 1915 – Deepening Conflict   27

3. 1916 – The Realization   45

4. 1916/17 – Seeing It Through   59

5. 1918 – The Final Blows   73

   Appendix   87

   Index   95

Acknowledgements

The author would like to extend her thanks to those who have helped with the compilation of this book. Nancy Tipton and family for sharing her mother's account of her experience's during the Great War, Hazel Crozier, curator at the RAF College Cranwell, for her help in sourcing photographs. Lincs To The Past, Lincolnshire County Council, an interesting source for those interested in the history of Lincolnshire. Jarrod Cotter for advice and photographs; also to Steven Blackah for his photographs and time.

Roni Wilkinson, Neil Barber and the rest of the team at Pen and Sword publishing for their support, and last, but not least, my family for their ongoing help and support in all aspects of life.

Introduction

The year 2014 saw the one hundredth anniversary of the start of the Great War, which began on 4 August 1914, when Britain declared war on Germany. Thousands of men endured difficult conditions overseas, and the casualties and fatalities were seemingly endless. What was expected to be a short period of conflict turned into years of fighting. Across our country, families worried about their loved ones whilst carrying on as best they could, considering the difficulties that presented themselves during this time. This book takes a brief look at how Lincoln, the county of Lincolnshire and its people fared during this period, the contribution made to the war effort and how life 'back home' evolved as the conflict continued.

The years prior to 1914 had been difficult, politically, due to the unrest across Europe. It had become obvious that there was a potential power struggle building, and that one country in particular was experiencing both turmoil internally, whilst looking to expand its borders elsewhere. With this in mind, Britain, France and Russia had signed a treaty offering support to each other in the event of conflict.

On 28 June 1914, Archduke Franz Ferdinand was assassinated in Sarajevo by Gavrilo Princip. However, this single event is deemed to be more of a trigger factor for the beginning of what was to become known as the Great War, rather than the actual cause. For the purposes of this book we will not delve too far into the politics of the time, preferring rather to focus on the events and people at home during these years.

CHAPTER ONE

1914 – Eager for a Fight

To many people in Britain who followed the politics of the nation on their radios and in some cases via the newspapers, the main cause of Britain declaring war on 4 August 1914 was the assassination of the Archduke, alongside the invasion of neutral Belgium, and the biggest fear was that Germany would carry on across the European countryside until it reached the French coast. The next target would then be England itself.

With a strong sense of patriotism, and keen to protect their country and prevent this happening, many men began enlisting even before the call to arms had been given. Confidence brimmed; with 'our boys' joining with the Allies we would soon rout the enemy and all would be over by Christmas.

Recruitment posts sprang up across the county and queues formed as groups of friends, families and workers waited to offer their services. Smaller towns and villages were visited, on a regular basis, by a group of recruiting officers who would set themselves up in the local village or Church hall until they had finished their recruiting drive. Enthusiasm was high, and as Lincoln was a garrison town with its own regimental barracks, it was not difficult to attract the young men of the city and surrounding areas. For those working in rural occupations the thought of joining up offered the opportunity to travel and for adventure that many could only have dreamed of.

Many of the county's inhabitants lived in poverty, and with large

THE OPENING OF THE ELECTRIC TRAMWAY, LINCOLN. 23.11.1905.

families and poor work prospects, the lure of a regular income was an incentive to many young men to join up.

Living in Lincolnshire, the obvious regiment of choice was the Lincolnshire Regiment, although recruitment was still carried out for other regiments depending on experience, numbers in the particular regiments, etc. As the years of conflict progressed, the recruitment offices would be tasked with increasing manpower in regiments that had suffered great losses and who were in need of more men to boost numbers. This saw local men in a variety of regiments based across the country. In small villages and hamlets in Lincolnshire, where the majority of men of enlisting age joined up, the effect was devastating and lead directly to poverty and hardship for the remaining family members during and post-war. Younger men, under the official age for enlistment, would often travel out of area in order to be recruited by people who would not recognize them and know they were underage and this often meant that they would be recruited into other regiments.

With no benefit system in place at that time, families cared for each other through good and bad times. Elderly, infirm parents joined the household of their children and were supported by them. Those families dependent on agriculture as an income were often struggling financially. Many were only employed, on a regular basis, during seasonal times of the year; for example, more manpower would be needed during harvest and potato picking time. Too many families found that there were times when finding work to provide an adequate income was virtually impossible, and even those workers with full time employment were frequently not paid enough to keep the family from suffering financial hardship. The situation was already causing unrest within the community, with debates and demonstrations becoming more commonplace long before the beginning of the Great War.

Large families were common, and with children leaving school aged fourteen, those families in very rural villages and hamlets found it almost impossible to find work. It is understandable that many of the boys who looked older than they were would try to enlist in order to bring much needed income into the home, but fathers would also enlist, perhaps in the hope that they would provide a steady income, and their sons may be able to fill positions left in the fields. It is debatable as to how many men in this situation joined up voluntarily, with the financial benefits being equally as important as their patriotism. As the months went on, and more men and teenagers joined up, the rural communities were beginning to struggle for manpower and we will take a look at the solutions to this problem later.

The Grimsby Chums

Lord Kitchener came up with a plan to increase the numbers of the Army without immediately bringing in conscription. He suggested that men who were joined by a common link, such as working in the same place, living in the same village or town, and those who shared common pursuits, could all join up together. This was an excellent plan, as it led to the men encouraging each other, and the recruiting offices began to be busy.

In some places large numbers of men were recruited, and if the majority of the battalion was from the same area, they were nicknamed 'Pals'; for example, The Barnsley Pals and the Accrington Pals.

In the Grimsby area posters were pasted across the town and surrounding villages. Printed by the Lincolnshire Regiment, the posters read, *'Wake up Grimsby! Young men do your duty. Join now with your pals. 500 men from all classes must be recruited at once.'*

The men of Grimsby responded immediately, bringing their friends, family and co-workers along with them. Men from other villages and towns near to Grimsby, such as Immingham, Caistor and Laceby, travelled to Grimsby to join up, and the ranks increased quickly. Joining up with someone that you knew made it more of an adventure, and let us not forget that when enough men were recruited, wherever that may be, village, town or city, they would march the men off to their training centres or to catch a train. It became a spectacle; English pomp and ceremony at its best, and one that boys and men alike aspired to be part of.

The men decided against using the term 'Pal' for what was to become the 10th Battalion, instead choosing to be known as The Grimsby Chums and they remained the only 'Pals' battalion to use the word 'Chums'.

As was the case across the country, supplies and armaments were not readily available for the new recruits. It was also difficult to find active commanding officers for the new battalions, and initially, retired Army personnel were recruited to lead the men during their basic training. Retired George Bennet, who had been Captain of the 1st Lincolnshire R.G.A. Volunteers, took charge of the recruits, but was soon to be replaced by George Heanage as a permanent C.O. to the battalion.

As well as the lack of supplies such as uniform and weapons, the battalion needed to be trained en masse, and facilities across the county were sparse. Once again the resourcefulness and enthusiasm of the Lincolnshire people for 'the cause' was evident as the Earl of Yarborough offered the grounds of his estate in and around Brocklesby as a training camp for the men. Offers of assorted weapons from the general public, and even old Post Office uniforms, helped the battalion to begin to feel a sense of unification, and training began in earnest during the winter of 1914. This was the community working together to help their own men to prepare for their forthcoming task. The pride that the communities had for the men going off to war was immeasurable; if they could not go, for whatever reason, then they supported those that could.

By Spring 1915, the men were kitted out properly with uniforms and weapons from the Army, and were ready for the next stage in their training, which was to be in Ripon, and here they were to sharpen their rifle skills before moving, yet again, to Wiltshire. By this time the Grimsby Chums had been joined by other men, and along with the Northumberland Fusiliers, Royal Scots and a battalion of the Suffolks, they made up the 34th Division.

It was not until 4 January 1916, that the Grimsby Chums were sent overseas, and had not only their first taste of life in the trenches, but also a visit from Kitchener himself, the man who had been instrumental in bringing the Chums together.

The Battle of the Somme, on 1 July 1916, was to be the first big offensive that the Chums were involved in, going forward to attack the village of La Boisselle. The men had been aware of the bombardment of the enemy lines and believed that once the signal for the advance was given, they would be able to easily overcome those, if any, remaining alive in the enemy trenches.

Unfortunately, this was not to be the case, and as the Grimsby Chums advanced, they were mown down by the German machine guns and mortar fire. Of the 1000 men, 15 officers and 487 men were killed, missing or wounded after the first few days of fighting.

Back home in Lincolnshire, the news was sadly received. In some families more than one member had lost their life or been seriously wounded. The future of the community began to look bleak, after all, it was the man who was the breadwinner, and without him what would the future hold? So many of the men that had joined the Grimsby Chums had been young men who left behind their wives, young children and babies and with approximately 600 of the Chums losing their lives during, or as a result of, the conflict, there was hardly a street or family that was not affected by the loss of family, friends or workmates. For example, Wintringham Grammar School was to lose eighty of its 'old boys'.

It has to be remembered that there was more than one way for a man to be affected by his time at the Front; men came home with wounds, amputations and suffering the after-effects of gas, which would affect their lungs and in some cases cause blindness or severe sight impairment. With such high casualty rates, there were men returning home all the time. Disability caused more hardship to the families, with many of the men not able to work and becoming dependent on their wives or parents to support them in practical and physical ways, as well as financially. There were of course, widow's pensions and invalidity pensions, however the system was not ideal, with various rules and regulations that sometimes made it impossible for someone to claim what they needed. Often, they would not be awarded an adequate pension, or even a pension at all, if an injury was not physically seen, and those with blindness or amputations were often passed on to charitable institutions such as St Dunstan's, which cared for those blinded during conflict. If awarded a pension, it was aimed to simply 'keep a man from destitution.'

It was of course, not just the physical injuries that were a problem for the men's families. Many men carried psychological wounds that would manifest in many ways such as violence, fear and inability to carry out simple tasks. These psychological impairments eventually became known as shell shock. We would recognize the condition today as Post Traumatic Stress Disorder. With the constant noise from bombardment, appalling living conditions within the trenches, fear for their lives twenty- four hours a day, and the stress of watching their friends, and in some cases family, being killed in front of them, it was not unreasonable to expect some sort of repercussions. Often, men with shell shock and no visible physical wounds would receive no pension at all. This made life, post-war, very difficult for everyone and would have certainly been the case for the families of the Grimsby Chums.

The worst thing for the families of the Chums was the uncertainty surrounding the fate of their loved ones. This of course, was the same for so many families right across the country. Unfortunately, due to the nature of the war, the families back home were receiving telegrams advising them that their family members were missing in action, which was no consolation to the family as the uncertainty was worse than certain knowledge that the soldier in question had died. Sometimes, that telegram would tell them that they were presumed dead and in some cases a letter from the commanding officer would follow confirming this. Communities were tight knit, supporting each other as they read lists of casualties posted on the parish notice board or similar, and as the war touched most families in one way or another, understanding and sympathy was on hand.

The uncertainty as to what had happened and the realization that your loved ones had not been buried, as their bodies had not been found, or in some cases there was no log of a burial as the paperwork had been lost, or the burials would have been so quick that there may not have been time to complete the relevant paperwork, was torture to the families. Let us also not forget that occasionally the Germans would actually bury the soldiers themselves in an act of compassion, and in that case, once again, there would be no record of the burial place. In these cases, the stories of that family member would be passed down, keeping the memory alive, but in an age where it has became commonplace for relations to travel overseas to visit graves and memorials, there is still great sadness at not knowing where that relation had been laid to rest.

In 2001, there was great excitement from the area that had been the battleground around Point du Jour on the Vimy Ridge. A mass grave had been uncovered containing the remains of twenty men, and close by, another grave, that of an officer. Archaeologists began to very carefully excavate the graves. However, they were disappointed to find that there were no personal items and no military artifacts either, such as cap badges, paperwork etc, which would immediately enable them to identify the men. Thankfully, although decades had passed, there were still some pieces of the uniforms on some of the men that were intact, and from one of these scraps the archaeologists identified the men as having served with the 10th Battalion, Lincolnshire Regiment, the Grimsby Chums.

Considering that there were records showing the loss of men from the 10th Battalion in such numbers that tallied with those found in the graves, it has been presumed that these were those men, but it has to be remembered that there were other battalions in this area and many of them also lost their lives, and their last resting places have also remained unknown.

The discovery of the graves has given the families of the missing

Grimsby Chums some sense of closure. With the popularity of tracing ancestors, developing family trees and unearthing the stories behind those relations, the effect of the Great War still has a very personal effect on families to this day, especially so with the commemorations of 100 years since the beginning of the Great War. The loss of a brother, cousin, father or son, has been passed through the generations, and if not felt personally, the hurt and upset of previous generations is still remembered and keenly felt.

At the end of the Great War, the colours of the Grimsby Chums was brought back to England, and in a service of remembrance, placed in the Parish Church to stand guardian over the memorial to those fine Grimsby men and their fellow soldiers. Although faded now, the bloody stains of conflict and suffering remain as witness to the courage and sacrifice of the men and to the courageous acceptance of the loss by those who remained behind.

The Youngest Recruit

Initially, there was no need for conscription, as by January 1915, there were a million voluntary recruits across the country. Conscription was, however, introduced in January 1916, as the loss of men was so great in such a short space of time that conscription was necessary to replace numbers in the Army. To begin with conscription was for single men aged eighteen to forty-one, (volunteers could enlist from the age of seventeen) and by May 1916, they had to extend the conscription to include married men. Although the rules specified that the men could not be younger than seventeen, and had to be at least five feet three inches tall, there were many occasions where birth certificates were 'lost' and the applicant's word was taken that they were of age. This happened right across the services, and with some of the boy's ages difficult to tell by sight alone, there were many very young boys recruited into the ranks, marching alongside men much older and perhaps somewhat more prepared emotionally than they were.

Lincolnshire boasts that the youngest recruit during the Great War came from the county; Private Sidney Lewis joined up in August 1915 and although he joined the East Surreys, joining up at Kingston, he actually came from Grantham.

By his thirteenth birthday, Sidney was on the Western Front, fighting on the Somme. Despite his young years, nobody could fault his bravery or keenness for the task in hand, and although only fighting for six weeks before his actual age was discovered, and he was sent home to be discharged, he had fought valiantly and was still awarded the Victory Medal and the British War Medal.

Sidney went on to join the Surry Police Force, having to wait until he was of the appropriate age this time.

There were those who were exempt from service, and whilst a farm owner was exempt from conscription, a farm labourer was not. It was possible to appeal to a tribunal for an exemption, and many were granted to those who were farm workers, especially in the early months of the conflict, as they worked in a job that was of national importance. However, as time went on, fewer exemptions were made on these grounds due to the huge losses and depletion of our Armed Forces.

Whilst the county's farms struggled under the reduction of workers, and therefore a reduction in vital production, there were those who went through the trouble of being granted an exemption only to enlist voluntarily due to feelings of guilt. Their conscience was often aided by being given a white feather, either directly or indirectly, frequently from ladies whose husbands, brothers or fathers were already fighting, or who had lost their lives. The feather was an indication of cowardice and was not just used within Lincolnshire; it was a trend across the country, sometimes most unjustly in the cases of those who were deemed medically unfit or who were in exempted occupations. On occasions, white feathers were passed over to servicemen home on leave whose uniforms were perhaps being washed by a diligent mother, and who was wearing civilian clothes.

Royal Naval Air Service, Cranwell

Seeing Royal Air Force aircraft flying overhead is an almost daily occurrence, depending on where you are within the county. Lincolnshire's close relationship with the RAF began during the Great War, continuing through the Second World War, up to the present day.

What is now known as RAF Cranwell came into service on 1 April 1916, under the command of Commodore Godfrey M. Paine. At the beginning of the Great War there was no Royal Air Force and the aircraft in military service came under the command of the Royal Naval

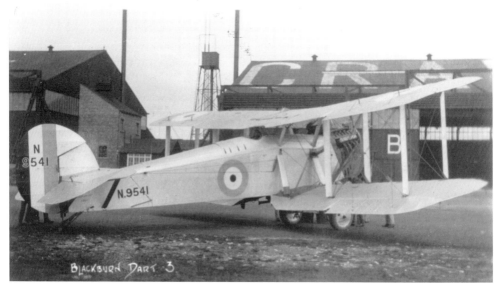

Ready for training at RNASC Cranwell. MOD Crown Copyright RAFC Cranwell

Air Service. The Admiralty realized that aircraft offered an early warning system should invasion be imminent, and so with that purpose in mind, as well as the role of defenders of the air, the Admiralty began setting up various stations on the south and east coast to establish a comprehensive network of airfields to defend the nation.

Lincolnshire's flat landscape was ideal for the relatively fast construction of air bases in both the First and Second World Wars, subsequently being nicknamed 'Bomber County' after the county's numerous RAF Stations 'homing' heavy bombers during the Second World War. Traditions has it that an airman was sent up to fly over the countryside in order to identify a piece of land that could be a potential site for a training airfield.

By mid-November 1915, construction was well underway on the 2,500 acre site to build a station with accommodation and other facilities to be found in huts rather than brick buildings, for ease and quickness of build, and with hangars being built to house aircraft and airships. The station had two runways running north and south, with training being offered for aircraft such as the Sopwith Camel, BE2cs, Avro 504s, airships and also the observation kite balloons that were invaluable as spotters during the conflict overseas. The kite balloons were used both on land and sea in order to offer updated information on how the conflict was evolving, on the enemy's position, and at sea, operating from ships, in order to act as submarine spotters. As a Naval facility, there was also training offered for other Naval trades more pertinent to working onboard a ship.

Smaller airfields were scattered across the Lincolnshire countryside, and by the end of the Great War there were thirty-seven airfields in the county. These had a range of purposes such as the small airfield not far away from Cranwell; RFC Anwick Landing Ground. [Insert Pic P1050559] The landing grounds gave the main airfields the advantage of being able to land their aircraft to re-fuel, re-arm and fly again, thus increasing the range and flying time and also offering a series of emergency landing sites. It must be remembered that the aircraft of the day were of very basic design and relatively fragile, easily damaged and not easily flown. Having the back up of a series of landing fields across the county must have offered some feeling of reassurance to those brave men flying as lookouts or endeavouring to shoot down the enemy airships.

Based a couple of miles from Anwick village, with access from Ruskington Fen Road, the airfield acted as an emergency and refuel/arming base. It was a small affair on fifty-four acres with a single electricity cable running into the village of Ruskington and no permanent buildings on site. There was a grass runway in the shape of a triangle, so that aircraft could land and take off, regardless of wind direction. Under the command of 38 Squadron, which flew BE2e and FE2b biplanes, the small group of men manning the aerodrome would fill in time between operations by helping the local farmers with whom they were frequently billeted.

In 1917, there was a major scare as a Zeppelin dropped nine bombs on the area surrounding RFC Anwick, however little damage was done other than large craters around Poplar Farm, which had many visitors from Ruskington and the surrounding area the following day, all coming to look at the craters and to be thankful that the airship had managed to miss any major constructions, be it civilian or Naval. It is interesting that an event such as this created such a ripple of interest. It shows how the local community, although regularly seeing 'our' aircraft overhead and knowing that there was a training school at Cranwell and the local landing site just down Ruskington Fen, was still so distanced from the reality of war that this event was cause for a trip out to see the damage. It was a novelty to the locals, although perhaps too close for comfort to the owners of Poplar Farm, which is now known as Ruskington Boarding Kennels, located on the outskirts of the village on the fen road.

The site of the airfield has long since been reclaimed by farmland. However, there remains a plaque commemorating RFC Anwick. The airfield closed after the end of the Great War, however it was opened again in September 1939 and acted as a decoy airfield for RAF Digby; flare lamps would be lit along the runway in an attempt to divert any bombers who were trying to target RAF Digby. The airfield was finally closed in August 1942.

This was not to be the only potentially dangerous local incident during that period. One of the more frightening accidents for local residents in and around Sleaford came in 1916 when, on a training flight, an airship crashed close to the town, proving that there was as much potential danger sited a few miles away from them, with the British airships seemingly as bad a culprits for accidents and loss of

Airship training at RNASC Cranwell. MOD Crown Copyright RAFC Cranwell.

life, as there was from possible enemy action. The benefits of RNAS Cranwell and its training role far outweighed the risks however, and proved invaluable in training pilots who were to serve either within this country or overseas.

Carrier Pigeons

Horses will always be associated with the Great War; thousands served and lost their lives. However, dogs also served along the trenches, passing messages to and fro and pigeons were also used.

There are records going back to the sixth century showing the use of pigeons to carry messages by the King of Persia, so using these birds was not a new innovation and their effectiveness had been proven over centuries.

Within the trenches there was a rudimentary system of communications. However, as the men advanced to new positions, or if the wires were cut by, for example, enemy shell fire, there would be a need to communicate with H.Q. Pigeons were an obvious choice. They were light to carry, swift in flight and the men were able to carry more than one in a lightweight wicker basket, normally carried on their backs.

The pigeons were kept in portable lofts, some were made out of London buses, and these would be transported closer to the lines, as and when necessary. Once the 'loft' had been in one place for a couple of weeks, the pigeons would automatically 'home' back to it. On arrival, they would trip a wire that rang a bell, signalling their arrival, and the message would then be removed from the small canister attached to their leg.

There are stories of the brave pigeons that made it back to the loft despite desperate wounds and in so doing saved the lives of many men at the cost of their own. No mean feat for a bird to be trying to fly home amongst shellfire, shrapnel and whilst being targeted by enemy fire as they attempted to bring down the bird carrying vital information back to the lines. The Germans also used pigeons to carry messages so were very aware that these birds could make the difference between which side would win that particular battle, hence targeting the birds when they saw them.

Back home in Lincolnshire another opportunity for the civilians to help those actively serving arose. With the use of carrier pigeons, and their unfortunate low survival rate, it was essential that the military had a good supply of proven pigeons. Racing pigeons was a national hobby, one that many men in Lincolnshire enjoyed, and birds were bred for stamina and speed, with the weaklings unfortunately being discarded.

Suddenly, across the country as well as Lincolnshire, a new sense of urgency arose in the lofts. It was now a matter of national importance that the pigeon owners bred their pigeons not to race across the country in order to win medals, but to be sent overseas to aid 'our boys'. The significance of breeding and co-operation between loft owners could mean the difference between life and death for a battalion of men. As each loft owner assessed their breeding stock, they must have been imagining loved ones with their lives at risk, depending on a pigeon carrying a message for help.

Pigeons continued to be used in the Second World War by airmen, seamen and soldiers with many Lincolnshire lofts, once again, providing outstanding birds fit for the task. Many of the birds, in both conflicts, were awarded medals for courage and for saving men's lives. Unfortunately, many of these were awarded posthumously. With advanced communication systems now in operation there has been no need for pigeons to be used in active service since the Second World War.

Life carries on

Whilst the conflict overseas was picking up apace, life in and around Lincoln was carrying on as normally as possible. There was still a general optimism that the war would be over soon and life continued as normally as possible, wherever it could.

Lincoln City Football club, for example, played on, adding to the illusion that all would be over soon. During the 1914/15 season, the team celebrated 225 home wins, 86 away wins, 57 score draws and 16 no-score draws.

The club had seen great success in the years prior to 1914, and in the 1911/12 season had won the Central League with what is still considered to this day to be one of Lincoln City Football Club's greatest teams; Fern, Jackson, Wilson, Robson, A. Gardner, T. Wield, J. Manning, M. Cubbin, W. Miller, Batty and Brindley. However, as the 1914/15 season went on, it was becoming more evident to all the clubs across the country that events overseas were not going to be coming to an end any time soon. In fact, so worried by the events was the club's committee that they actually closed the gates during an F.A. Cup second round, second replay, so that vital ammunition workers would not be tempted to leave their work. With conscription beginning to take effect, many professional players across the country had either voluntarily enlisted or were about to be conscripted. Opinions varied as to whether or not the professional players should actually be classed as having a reserved occupation, in order to keep morale up at home, or whether they should be on active service, as they were obviously fit and healthy young men.

As more professional players joined up (of the 5,000 professional players across the country over 2,000 joined up) the decision was eventually taken to suspend all competitive football across the country, a decision that stood until 1919 when the clubs began to reform their teams. In order to retain some semblance of normality, regional leagues were set up with results not counting when the national leagues began again. Guest players travelled across the country, joining the various teams. Players such as Brendel Anstey and Daniel Tremelling guested at Lincoln F.C., however none of the players, professional or amateur, would receive credit for any of the matches played during this period. This was to ensure that those who were overseas and able to restart their football careers once the hostilities ended, would start on an equal footing. These regional matches were a good morale booster and did, at the very least, give some semblance of normality to Lincoln City F.C. supporters.

The smaller village leagues were also suspended until the end of the Great War, with the last final being played in 1914 between Metheringham and Waddington, with Waddington emerging the victors with a 2-1 win.

CHAPTER TWO

1915 – Deepening Conflict

The optimism of the early days of the Great War was slowly waning. The belief that hostilities would have ceased by Christmas 1914 had been bitterly shattered and the British people were beginning to come to terms with what was really happening overseas, and to resign themselves to rallying around each other to give support and comfort, and to find ways to help the war effort, whilst coming directly under attack themselves at times.

William Foster & Co design the First Tank

Conditions overseas were atrocious; the biggest problem hampering our troops was the mud, which was everywhere. Horses were struggling to pull the heavy artillery guns into position, and trying to advance on foot whilst coping with deep mud and under fire, was increasing the risk of fatalities and casualties.

Although the Army did already have some armoured vehicles, they could not cope with the problems that trench warfare presented, and in 1914 Lieutenant Colonel Ernest Swinton assessed the situation and began to champion the design and introduction of a vehicle that could cope with the new terrain. The Admiralty Landships Committee was formed to debate and progress the possibility of developing a machine that would help reduce fatalities and bring an end to the war.

After great debate, the committee decided on certain criteria that the machine had to meet, which were as follows:

Have a top speed of 4mph on flat land.
Be able to turn sharply at top speed.
Be able to climb a five-foot parapet.
Be able to cross an eight-foot gap.
Have a working radius of twenty miles.

Operate with a crew of ten men, using two on-board machine guns and an artillery gun.

The Army was already using Lincoln company, William Foster and Co's caterpillar- tracked tractor, in order to move the heavy howitzer guns into place. The caterpillar track coped well with the difficult terrain, and the government could see the potential of this design and decided to take it further. With a working relationship already in place with the company, the committee decided to ask William Foster and Co to design, in utmost secrecy, a prototype machine that could work under their criteria.

William Tritton had joined the company in 1905, a talented man, well able to carry the company forward on a business level, but also with his own design ideas.

When the company was asked to become involved in the project, the Admiralty Landships Committee seconded Walter Wilson, member of the Royal Navy Armoured Car Section, to the company to work closely alongside William Tritton in designing the new vehicle. Wilson had already developed a reputation for designing vehicles, including armoured vehicles, and with his experience of handling equipment like this, the partnership was to be fruitful.

The other vital member on the design team was William Rigby, whose talent was in the drawing up of designs. He could put a man's vision down accurately on to paper. He could put a man's vision down on paper, bringing it almost to life in the process.

Due to the demand for secrecy, the design team decided that regular meetings at the factory may draw attention to them, so they decided to meet in a room at a local hotel called the White Hart. The hotel is

Plaque commemorating the
life of Sir William Tritton

Tanks in various stages of manufacture. © Lincs to the Past, Lincs County Council

still in existence today, situated in Bailgate, Lincoln, close to the Cathedral and the Castle.

A name was needed for the project, and as the initial design for the main body of the vehicle resembled a water tank, the nickname 'tank' was given to the project. As the design progressed and came into fruition, the name stuck and to this day, this type of armoured vehicle is still called a tank.

It did not take long for the first prototype to roll off the factory floor, and trials were carried out on South Common, Lincoln. By 22 September 1915, the team was happy with their tank, and 'Little Willie' was named.

Following Little Willie came the much larger

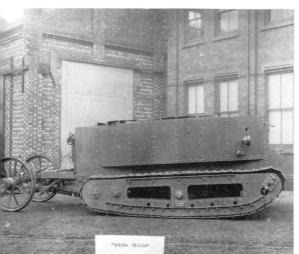

Little Willie outside the firm's office. © Lincs to the Past, Lincs County Council

"Little Willie"

version, conforming to the Admiralty's specifications, nicknamed 'Big Willie'.

The first operational tanks arrived in Europe on 30 August 1916, and then the task of training crews began in earnest ready for the tanks to take their place in their first Front Line action in the attack on Flers.

In 1917, William Tritton was knighted for his services in designing and building the first tanks. It will come as no surprise to discover that Tritton Road, Lincoln, was named in his honour.

Walter Wilson went back to the Army, becoming a Major in the newly formed Tank Corps, where he was twice mentioned in dispatches and became a companion of the Order of St Michael and St George in 1917.

In 1919, Tritton and Wilson were recognized for their work on the tank design and awarded £15,000 to share between them, as decided by the Royal Commission. Tritton chose not to keep his share, considering his knighthood to be sufficient praise, and instead gave his share to the workers who had played such a pivotal role in the manufacturing of the first tanks.

Zeppelin Raids

The country was coming under regular attack from bombing raids by the Germans. However, this was via airships rather than aircraft. These large airships could silently cross the country, at approximately eighty-five miles per hour, in many cases dropping their bomb load without any prior notice being given to the communities beneath them. Airships helped the Germans maintain the element of surprise and also offered the ability to carry large bomb loads of up to two tons, thus ensuring the maximum impact per trip, with incendiary bombs being a favourite. The bombing raids began early in 1915.

Although there were air bases across Lincolnshire tasked with defending against these airships, it was often too late to intercept them. The other problem that the aircraft had with the Zeppelins was that the craft was made up of compartments filled with hydrogen, which was very flammable, however there had to be a spark in order to ignite the gas. The ammunition fired from 'our' aircraft would simply travel through the airship and continue out the other side with only small holes made, which were not large enough to deflate the compartments and bring down the airship.

It was only when new ammunition was specifically designed that gave an actual spark, and subsequent flame as the bullet travelled into the airship, that the attacks against these massive invaders became more successful.

It was debatable as to whether there were specific targets identified in and around Lincoln, or whether the Zeppelins had been blown off their original target due to adverse weather conditions, something that was quite common due to the nature of the airship.

Lincoln itself came under attack, possibly due to its connection with tank and aircraft production. However, attacks on Navenby, Skellingthorpe and other smaller villages may well be attributed to bad navigation or high winds blowing the airships off course, and the crew's determination to drop the bombs.

During one night attack, on 16 September 1916, it is said that a train driver spotted a Zeppelin, which appeared to be following the course of the train with the intention of being led into the centre of Lincoln. The quick-thinking driver halted the train just before arriving in the city, and the Zeppelin was totally duped into dropping all his bombs into a Washingborough garden and the surrounding fields, with no injuries being sustained. The story is well remembered locally and commemorated in a stained glass window within the Church of St John in Washingborough itself.

Unfortunately, not all Zeppelin raids were without injury. One raid on the Lincolnshire coast cost the lives of thirty-one members of the 3rd Battalion of the Manchester Regiment, when their billet, a Baptist Church, took a direct hit from one of the bombs.

It is estimated that by the end of the Great War, over 1500 British citizens had died as a direct result of Zeppelin raids.

Caring for the wounded in Lincoln

The numbers of wounded were increasing rapidly overseas, and it became obvious that in order to cope with the numbers, that the injured would have to be sent back 'home' to hospitals and convalescent homes. Even those whose injuries would not see them invalided out of the Army would be sent home to heal and recuperate before being sent overseas again, and in many cases this would be without being given the opportunity to visit family, despite being in the same country.

There were hospitals of varying sizes set up across the country. Depending on the size of the facility, they would be manned by Royal Army Medical Corps staff, Queen Alexandra's Imperial Military Nursing Service working alongside voluntary organizations such as the Red Cross, St. John's Ambulance, YMCA, and the VAD (Voluntary Aid Detachment).

Large hospitals were set up according to region, and Lincoln came under the Northern Command area, being one of five hospitals; 1st Northern General Hospital (Newcastle), 2nd Northern General Hospital (Leeds), 3rd Northern General Hospital (Sheffield), 4th Northern General Hospital (Lincoln) and the 5th Northern General Hospital (Leicester).

The Army requisitioned the Lincoln Grammar School on Wragby Road in Lincoln, and this was to become known as the 4th Northern General Hospital. It was a large building with the facilities to treat 41 officers and 1126 other ranks. Over the course of the Great War, the 4th Northern General treated over 45,000 men. It was a general hospital, treating a wide range of medical problems, and from here, patients could be transferred across to other units specializing, for

Wounded soldiers in convalescent uniform and nurses outside one of the temporary buildings at 4th Northern General Hospital. Copyright Lincs to the Past, Lincs County Council

One of the wards at Fourth Northern General Hospital. © Lincs to the Past, Lincs County Council

Outside the Fourth Northern General Hospital; the King decorating some of the men. © Lincs to the Past, Lincs County Council

example, in treating amputees, those blinded by gas or shrapnel and those with psychological problems.

The grounds of the school were also put to good use in order to maximize the amount of personnel that the hospital could accept. Wooden huts were built on what had been the sports fields. These substantial buildings had all the usual utilities that enabled them to be used as additional wards. Neighbouring households complained of the noise, as the construction of these extra wards carried on throughout the night, such was the urgency, and need, for these extra beds.

The men that arrived at the hospital had been through a series of hospitals or 'stations' closer to the Front, although many of these were tented units rather than brick buildings. It was a complicated series of examinations and reports that eventually led a soldier to be sent back to Britain for recovery and further treatment. If injured on the Front Line, the soldier would immediately be seen by the respective Battalion Medical Officer(s), orderlies, or stretcher-bearers, with all of the latter trained in first aid, and if the injury was insignificant, then they would be treated then and there, and returned to their post in the trenches.

The Advanced Dressing Stations were there to treat those who required more attention, and minor operations were carried out here. Men could still recover from the Advanced Dressing Station and be sent back to the Front Line, or they could go straight to one of the Casualty Clearing Stations, which were equipped to deal with those who required major operations such as amputations. Men could be sent from there, and from the Advanced Dressing Station, to the Base Hospital, where some of them would be evacuated to Britain, once deemed well enough to travel.

The transportation of the men was not easy. If they were categorized as walking wounded, then they would be walked from one station to another. Horse drawn wagons would provide transport for those not able to walk and in some areas there were light railways and barges (where possible) that had been set up to transport provisions, ammunitions and the wounded along the lines. It is hard to imagine having to endure miles in a horse drawn wagon, across rutted ground whilst recovering from an amputation or serious shrapnel wound. These stations would also be used if the men were ill, and with dysentery a frequent killer, it was not unusual to be transporting sick men as well as the wounded.

Once in England, the troops would be sent to a military hospital or convalescent home, depending on the severity of their injuries. This was not always close to home and it was often the case that relatives were informed, or the soldier wrote himself, that they were in the country and receiving treatment, but due to financial and logistical problems the family was not able to visit. How frustrating must it have been for a poverty-stricken family from a Lincolnshire hamlet to know that their son or husband was in the country and yet too far away for them to visit. This became even more poignant when, in many cases, the soldier recovered sufficiently to be sent back to the Front without a leave pass, only to be fatally wounded and never to return. What angst must have been felt at the lost opportunity for one last meeting?

The hospital was not the only one to be found in Lincoln and the surrounding area; the Drill Hall, which was originally built by Joseph Ruston in 1889/90 as a venue for the Lincoln Volunteers to train, was also turned into a hospital. Brocklesby Hall near Grimsby had become an auxiliary hospital, as had Boultham Park Hall, Lincoln, and Belton House near Grantham. The landed gentry frequently volunteered their large houses, halls and estates to become either auxiliary hospitals or convalescent homes, with some preferring to specifically cater for officers, whilst others took men of all ranks.

It was sometimes as a direct result of opening part of the house up to the wounded that the women of these more affluent families gained their first taste of gainful employment, albeit unpaid, and thus encouraged many of these young women who went on to volunteer in the VAD, and post-war, to find jobs of their own, rather than being kept by a father or husband. The social system was forever changed by the events of the Great War.

There were male and female nurses in the hospitals and convalescent homes, many of them part of the VAD, Voluntary Aid Detachment. It fell to each County's branch of the Red Cross to train the local volunteers in basic nursing and first aid skills. Lincolnshire's headquarters of the Red Cross, based in Boston, organized the other branches across the county. By the end of 1914, there were 74,000 volunteers across the country, offering not only nursing skills, but able to work anywhere that their individual skills would help, for example office and kitchen work.

There were also trained nurses who were employed to work in the homes and hospitals, and the 4th Northern General Hospital had the very efficient Matron Shepherd, who was employed as Matron of Lincoln County Hospital, acting as Principal Departmental Matron. This lady soon had the 4th Northern running like clockwork, and to her credit, she still held her position as Matron of the County Hospital too. As Immediate Matron, operating under Matron Shepherd, was Miss Baildon.

By mid September 1914, the hospital received its first patients directly from the Front. One hundred and five men arrived with varying injuries, including amputations. These men were the injured from the Battle of Mons, who had arrived at Southampton and once stabilized, transferred to Lincolnshire for further treatment, convalescence and recovery, depending on their injuries. Transportation of the men to Lincoln from the various ports was relatively easy as Lincoln had the train station, which could receive the men and allow them to travel in relative comfort, especially considering the means of transport closer to the Front.

By the end of October, the hospital was full, not only with English soldiers, but also with Belgian soldiers too, who shared the wards alongside the English, each having fought alongside each other.

It became apparent that the men, of whatever nationality, needed additional supplies. In many cases they had arrived with only the clothes that they stood in, and Matron Shepherd organized a clothes drive, asking the local people for any clothes that they did not need to be donated. The Lincoln people rallied with gusto, happy to be involved in doing something practical that would have a direct effect on the soldiers that had fought so valiantly, and before long the hospital had a plentiful supply of clothes.

Matron Shepherd was not the only one asking for donated clothing. The Red Cross organized clothes drives in order to accumulate a store of clothes for the county's main and smaller hospital facilities, and also to send overseas. With local braches spread across the county, the response was equal to that found by Matron Shepherd when she requested help from the people of Lincoln. The terrible conditions overseas often meant that men lost spare clothing or that it was beyond repair. In many cases the clothing being sent overseas would have belonged to a man who had served and lost his life, an irony indeed.

Not only were English and Belgian soldiers treated and cared for in Lincolnshire, the Americans were also a major presence in the county; the large former Nocton Hall, at Nocton, was turned into a hospital and given to the Americans to be used as a hospital for their officers in 1917. The hall was used as a hospital until the Americans handed it back to the British. The hall went on to be used as a hospital during the Second World War and was also made ready to receive the injured from the Gulf War.

Specialist hospitals and convalescent homes were set up across the county. These catered for those injured soldiers with specific conditions such as shell shock, amputees, and those blinded in action. Obviously, the blind and amputees would never be able to return to active service. However, those men in hospital or convalescent homes who were deemed fit by the medical staff, would make the long trip to the

Command Depot in Ripon where they would then be sent back to their original regiments, or in some cases where the regiment had sustained many casualties and been disbanded, sent to another one, or return to the Front to find very few, if any familiar faces.

The Lincoln Regiment

The Lincoln Regiment was founded on 20 June 1685, and was originally named The Earl of Bath's Regiment of Foot. The first Colonel of the Regiment was the Earl of Bath, John Granville, and one of the first recorded major conflicts that the Regiment was to be involved in was the Nine Years War, 1688 to 1697.

In 1751, there was a major overhaul of the British Army's naming of regiments, and each regiment was given a number. The Earl of Bath's Regiment became known as the 10th Regiment of Foot.

The 10th Regiment remained operational in varying conflicts overseas, returning to England in 1778, after nineteen long years abroad. It was to be 1881 when the Regiment was formally linked with the county of Lincolnshire, primarily a strategy to encourage enlistment. Pride in country and county was promoted and used to increase the number of the regiment.

After a successful campaign in Egypt, where the regiment fought during the Napoleonic Wars, under the overall command of Wellington, the regiment was given the Sphinx as part of their badge. Another conflict overseas, this time in India during the Anglo-Sikh War, 1846 – 49, saw the regiment being awarded for gallantry in combat, their service also being remembered by the naming of the Regimental Headquarters as Sobraon Barracks, after their actions at the Battle of Sobraon on 10 February 1846, part of the Sikh Wars, with the green area behind the barracks in Lincoln being called Sobraon Park.

In 1774, the Regiment sailed from a posting in Ireland, across to America where the soldiers were to fight in the War of Independence, seeing action in many places, including Bunker Hill and Long Island.

There were of course, many other conflicts that the regiment took part in, and the above are only a few mentioned by way of example of the regimental activities prior to the Great War. It should also be noted that the men were nicknamed 'Yellowbellies', a common term used to describe Lincolnshire people. There are many reasons offered for this

Modern-day photograph of Sabraon Barracks

fondly used term, that is still in use today, such as the regimental dress included a waistcoat with yellow braid, or perhaps the association with the women of the county whose aprons would stain yellow as they harvested mustard, even a link with a frog or a lizard with a yellow stomach area. Whatever the derivation of the term, it is used with pride, and I personally, am very proud to be a Lincolnshire Yellowbelly!

The regiment also sported the name 'The Poachers'. This was taken from a popular song that was linked to the county and used as an unofficial anthem. It has to be remembered that during the years when the Regiment was first set up, poaching was rife due to poverty across the county, and many were caught stealing rabbits, pheasants and suchlike in order to keep their family fed. Children would be taught how to set snares, and in the records at Lincoln Castle, there are children, not even in their teens, who are recorded as being held for poaching. In some cases the option to join the local regiment was offered, and taken, in place of a jail sentence or deportation. This all added even more to the relevance of the song, and the lyrics are shown below.

The Lincolnshire Poacher

When I was bound apprentice in famous Lincolnshire
'Twas well I served my master for nigh on seven years
Till I took up to poaching as you shall quickly hear
Oh, 'tis my delight on a shiny night in the season of the year.
As me and my companions was setting out a snare
'Twas then we spied the gamekeeper, for him we didn't care
For we can wrestle and fight, my boys, and jump from anywhere
Oh, 'tis my delight on a shiny night in the season of the year.
As me and my companions was setting four or five
And taking them all up again, we caught a hare alive
We caught a hare alive, my boys, and through the woods did steer
Oh, 'tis my delight on a shiny night in the season of the year.
We threw him over my shoulder, boys, and then we trudged home
We took him to a neighbour's house and sold him for a crown
We sold him for a crown, my boys, but I divven't tell you where
Oh, 'tis my delight on a shiny night in the season of the year.
Success to every gentleman that lives in Lincolnshire
(Alt. Bad luck to every magistrate that lives in Lincolnshire)
Success to every poacher that wants to sell a hare
Bad luck to every gamekeeper that will not sell his deer
Oh, 'tis my delight on a shiny night in the season of the year.

It was a rousing sight to watch the new recruits, ready to join their fellow 'Yellowbellies' in the trenches, heads held high, with their families and friends cheering them on as they attempted to march in time to the song.

Music played an important part during the Great War, as it has done during other conflicts. Songs could soothe and comfort those who were homesick, ill or wounded, they could raise a soldier's spirits as they stood knee deep in mud waiting for that inevitable whistle to blow to signal the start of a push forward. How many times did one of 'our' 'Yellowbellies' begin to sing the regimental song, encouraging others to join in? Perhaps a tentative chorus at first, building as the men's spirits, and adrenalin, soared. A small link with home, conjuring up the images of flat fenland interspersed with woods, fields full of potatoes, cabbages and brussel sprouts; rich, dark soil, freshly ploughed and that inevitable pheasant strutting along the field side with his winter plumage shining against the frost covered soil. The vision of home would encourage the soldiers to battle on, fighting for their country and specifically their county, Lincolnshire, where their families waited for them to come home victorious.

A total of nineteen battalions of the regiment saw battle during the Great War and the King's Colours bears witness to the courage and honour in which they served. The Royal Anglian and Royal Lincolnshire Regimental Association list the Battle Honours for the Lincolnshire Regiment as follows:

Mons	*Le Cateau*	*Retreat from Mons*
Marne 1914	*Aisne 1914 1918*	*La Bassée 1914*
Messines '14 '17 '18	*Armentiéres 1914*	*Ypres 1914, 1915, 1917*
Nonne Bosschen	*Neuve Chappelle*	*Gravenstafel*
St. Julien	*Frezenberg*	*Bellewaarde*
Aubers	*Loos*	*Somme 1916, 1918*
Albert 1916, 1918	*Bazentin*	*Delville Wood*
Poziéres	*Flers-Courcelette*	*Morval*
Thiepval	*Ancre 1916, 1918*	*Arras 1917, 1918*
Scarpe 1917, 1918	*Arleux*	*Pilckem*
Langemarck 1917	*Menin Road*	*Polygon Wood*
Broodseinde	*Poelcappelle*	*Passchendaele*
Cambrai 1917, 1918	*St Quentin*	*Bapaume 1918*
Lys	*Estaires*	*Bailleul*
Kemmel	*Amiens*	*Drocourt Quéant*
Hindenburg Line	*Epéhy*	*Canal du Nord*
St Quentin Canal	*Beaurevoir*	*Selle*
Sambre	*France & Flanders 1914 – 1918*	
Suvla	*Landing at Suvla*	*Scimitar Hill*
Gallipoli 1915	*Egypt 1916*	

There is a comprehensive list of all actions taken by the Lincolnshire Regiment during the Great War in the Appendix at the back of the book, which makes for interesting reading. However, those listed above were especially recognized with honour. Alongside the honours, there were three Victoria Crosses awarded, perhaps little compensation for the estimated 8,800 casualties that the regiment sustained during the Great War.

The men awarded the Victoria Cross gained their medals in different actions and of the three men only one was actually a Lincolnshire man. We shall look at the others first.

Captain Percy Howard Hansen of the 6th Battalion was only 24 years old, serving in Gallipoli, when he was involved in a battle in Yilghin Bumu on 9 August 1915. The fighting had been hard and the battalion was forced to retreat, leaving wounded behind due to heavy fire and the scrubland being set alight. Captain Hansen was appalled at the situation and the thought of the wounded being caught in the fire and literally burning to death, so he took a handful of volunteers and, under enemy fire, went back to rescue six of the wounded.

Captain Hansen was Danish and survived the Great War, going on to see service during the Second World War.

Sergeant Arthur Evans from Seaforth, was 27 years old and a member of the 6th Battalion, Lincolnshire Regiment. At the time of the action that saw him awarded the Victoria Cross, he was using the name of Walter Simpson. He was originally a member of the 1st Kings Liverpool Regiment. Records do not indicate how he went on to become a member of the 6th Battalion, but he was a brave man who received his medal for his actions during the fighting at Etaing, France.

Single-handedly, he overwhelmed a key sentry position manned with a machine gun, killing two enemy soldiers and causing four more to surrender after first swimming a river. With the machine-gun post out of action, a patrol, including Sergeant Evans, proceeded to advance across the river, however they came under heavy fire and one of the officers was wounded. With no thought to his own safety, Sergeant Evans helped the officer back to safety under heavy enemy fire.

Arthur Evans did survive the Great War, however his health was compromised due to gas inhalation. He died aged 45, in Sydney, Australia.

The third recipient of the Victoria Cross in the Lincolnshire Regiment was from Lincolnshire itself. Acting Corporal Charles Richard Clarke was born in Pickworth, a small village close to Folkingham, Sleaford. His was the typical story of farmer's son who preferred the excitement and promised adventure to that of staying at home, helping his father with the family farm. In 1905, at the young age of 16, and before the beginning of the Great War, he joined the Lincolnshire Regiment, being placed in the 2nd Battalion, where he was to remain during the conflict on the Western Front.

On 9 May 1915, a major 'push' towards Rouges Bancs began,

unfortunately an action that would lead to many casualties and fatalities. However, initially morale was high as the soldiers went over the top. Corporal Clarke did not go over in the first wave of troops, as two companies of the Lincolnshires had been reserved as reinforcements if necessary.

It became evident that the bombardment of the enemy placements had not been as successful as first thought, and the first wave of soldiers were placed under heavy fire and began to retreat. Brigadier General Cole sent the last two companies out in the hope of bolstering their fellow soldiers in order to complete the advance. Corporal Clarke was in one of the hand-bombing parties. These hand bombs were frequently made from empty tin cans containing gunpowder, stones and a fuse. They were effective enough, however a degree of courage was needed in the making and transporting of these devices even before they lit the fuse. (As the Great War progressed, safer 'bombs' and grenades were designed).

With determination and great courage, Corporal Clarke advanced on the enemy position and single-handedly cleared a 50-foot section of trench line. Joined by four other members of the company, he then went on to clear and hold another 250-foot trench line.

The troops were called to retreat later in the day. However, for courage and determination during the action, he was awarded the Victoria Cross.

Corporal Clarke survived the Great War, staying in the Army until 1928, when he left having reached the rank of Master Sergeant. He returned to Lincolnshire, working in and around Bourne, and became well known for his presence at the Remembrance Services each year, and also for maintaining the Memorial Gardens.

There were other servicemen in the Lincoln Regiment who also received medals commemorating their courage and bravery under fire; many were posthumously awarded, which gave the family scant comfort. It is not possible to mention everyone in this book,

Two gentlemen from the
Lincolnshire Regiment
on a period postcard.

however that does not detract from the importance and courage of their actions.

The Lincolnshire Regiment took part in many actions; all would have been reported in the national and local press.

For those not able to afford a newspaper, casualty lists and main headlines were published in a prominent position for all to see. Even a brief look at the long list of actions at the back of this book gives the reader a certain understanding of the ongoing conflict that 'our boys' were involved in, and how the Lincolnshire families of those serving must have literally held their breath between letters from their loved ones. Even a telegram or letter informing them of injury was felt as a relief; perhaps the injury was enough to ensure that 'he' would be invalided out of the Army or given a job at home rather than on the Front. Unfortunately, too often the men were 'mended and moved out' and the worrying began again.

Edith Smith - First Policewoman

Lincolnshire had the same problems that were to be found across the country where military camps and training grounds were to be found; the troops attracted women of 'ill-repute', keen to socialize with the men and relieve them of some of their pay. It was also common to find generally respectable women who were led astray whilst their husbands were fighting overseas.

Trying to cope by yourself, missing your husband who had been at the Front for months, was a lonely task, despite having family nearby, and many of these family women were easy targets for a smooth talking man in a uniform, especially one who was generous with his pay.

Unfortunately, the Armed Forces were beginning to find that there was another enemy silently creeping amongst its ranks, debilitating, and in some cases killing the men, urgently needed to be healthy and fighting on the Front Line. This killer was venereal disease, and was to be found in every hospital unit on the Front. There were also cases of men being evacuated back to Britain, as the disease had taken such a hold and they were so ill. There must have been such shame in being medically

Studio portrait of Mrs Edith Smith, first paid policewoman in the country. © Lincs to the Past, Lincs County Council

removed from service due to a sexually contracted disease, especially when the 'victim' was a married man. It was estimated that at one time, over 55,000 men had cases of VD.

In Grantham, the problem of prostitution, and also of married women with families taking up with the troops, was no different to the rest of the country. However, the authorities were determined to do something about it. With camps at Belton and Harrowby, the town attracted many soldiers on their days off. The police force already had some volunteer women police officers, however they did not hold the position or have the authority that their fellow male officers had. It seemed that what was needed was a woman who could relate to the women whilst having the power of arrest. With this in mind, Edith Smith (one of the first women to have joined the Women's Police Volunteers) was sworn in at the Guidhall in August 1915, and with full powers of arrest, she became the first paid policewoman in the country.

Edith worked relentlessly; her role was to work with the women and children of the town, and such was her dedication to her job that she worked seven days a week until she left the police force two years later. She had a unique way about her, using her powers of arrest as a last resort, preferring instead to try and talk the women out of fraternizing and prostitution.

She thought nothing of knocking on doors where she thought the wife of a serving soldier may be entertaining a gentleman friend. Many of the town's soldiers would seek her out prior to leaving for active service and ask her to keep an eye on their wife, as they suspected she may be unfaithful whilst they were away.

Edith knew the parts of the town where the prostitutes would 'work' and the quiet areas that a couple would go to find somewhere to be together, and she patrolled these areas with determination. She also dealt with other crimes, such as theft, that involved women and children.

Edith resigned after two years of diligent service and went on to marry and have a family, although sadly to die six years later after an overdose of morphine. There is a road in Grantham named after her as a memorial to Britain's first female police officer.

CHAPTER THREE

1916 – The Realization

1916 began in the same way that 1915 had; despite the bravado of the early months of the Great War, there appeared to be no end in sight, and the losses by now were increasing at a rapid rate. Across the county, families were mourning the loss of their loved ones and coming to the realization that life would never be the same again; from the landed gentry through to the poorest families, the notifications were the same, as was the reaction.

Daily life carried on as well as it could with reduced manpower and daily uncertainty with the effects of the conflict rippling across the country touching every family in different ways.

Zeppelin Attack

Some of the more rural villages came under attack from enemy airships, and it was hard for the people to understand why they were targeted. For example, on the evening of 31 January 1916, the railway station at Sleaford was telegraphed and told of a Zeppelin that was making its way across country on a direct path towards the town. Immediately, the call went up to extinguish all lights,

Territorials marching off prior to embarkation to France. © Lincs to the Past, Lincs County Council

which would make it difficult for the airship to recognize the town as a target. Was the airship en route to Cranwell? Was it searching for Lincoln in order to target the factories there, or was it simply lost, having been searching for a larger target and trying to find a place to offload its bombs?

Sleaford was lucky and avoided being bombed, however the small village of Digby was to take a direct hit from one of the bombs, which seemed to be one of a handful dropped over the Digby and Bloxholm area. The only damage done on this occasion was to a barn in Church Street, which was set alight by an incendiary bomb dropping onto bags inside the barn. The fire was soon put out and no serious damage done.

The incident was reported to the local police, and Inspector Skipworth from Metheringham came out and recorded the incident, noting that the fire was soon under control and no other damage was reported in the area. It has to be remembered that at this point the airfield at Digby was just being set up, and not as high profile an airfield as it was to become during the next war, and so highly unlikely that the airfield was the target.

Welbourn was the next target; again with incendiary bombs being dropped, as the expectation was that these bombs would burst into flame, burn for some length of time, setting alight anything and everything around them, thus causing maximum damage. Thankfully, no damage was done.

The Zeppelins were the silent stalkers of the night; after bombs being dropped in places of little or no importance, the Lincolnshire people became wary and frightful. Was nobody safe? However, being made of 'stern stuff', daily life carried on and the harder life became, the more determined the people were to ride out the hardship and threats, and to survive until 'we' won the war.

Blackout rules were in place, and officers would patrol making sure that the rules were enforced.

The Army Remount Service

The Army Remount Service was established in 1887 as a means to control and regulate the purchasing of horses of good condition, age and fitness. Prior to this, it had been the responsibility of individual regiments and their representatives to purchase new stock, however this meant that prices and condition of animals fluctuated from regiment to regiment.

In 1891, the Remount Service became part of the Army Service Corps (ASC) and in 1914, four main Remount Units were established across the country; at Woolwich, Melton Mowbray, Dublin and Arborfield. Horses were not only acquired from the Home Counties, but bought and imported from Ireland, North and South America, Spain and Portugal. There were four main depots that were able to deal with the horses and supplies; Shirehampton, (for horses received at Avonmouth), Romsey (Southampton), Ormskirk (Liverpool) and Swaythling, which gathered together all of the horses trained at the other sites and shipped across the Channel to begin their Army careers.

468,323 horses were compulsorily purchased during the war years within the United Kingdom alone, and with Lincolnshire being such a rural county, the Remount Service soon arrived.

Each farm was visited, the horses logged and assessed as to age, size and condition, followed by purpose and necessity to that particular farm, smallholding or estate. The larger estates and farms were to lose their hunters immediately, as hunting was deemed a sporting pastime, and therefore these animals in prime condition were not necessary to the daily running of the establishments to which they belonged. This, naturally, saw a decline in hunting across the county, as there were not the horses of suitable condition and quality to meet the requirements of a hunter. In some places hunt meetings were halted, whilst others attempted to keep going with infrequent meetings, shortened to take into account the availability and condition of horses. Many men joined cavalry units, taking their favourite hunter with them.

Larger riding horses and those horses used to pull carriages were not essential for a household, and sacrifices had to be made, it was deemed tolerable. The general rule of thumb was that horses from 15.2 to 16 hands were considered as light draught horses, and these were essential to the Cavalry, and also to pull light artillery equipment, ambulances, stores wagons etc. These horses proved invaluable to the war effort and were used throughout the Western Front.

The Army also needed heavy horses to pull the larger guns and provisions, and so the attention turned to the farmers and their stock. It was to be a fine line between allowing a farmer to keep enough horses to allow him to run his farm on a daily basis, and in some cases a farmer may be left with one horse, which would be expected to do all the jobs on the farm, and that horse may well be older. If the farm produced a small amount of milk that could be taken by hand cart to be delivered, rather than using their cart and only horse, then the Army would procure that horse.

The relationship between the farmers in Lincolnshire and the Remount Service was bittersweet, as it was across the country. There was, on the one hand, resentment that they had taken away an animal on which their livelihood may depend, however, on the other hand, the Army also required provisions for their animals, and would happily buy hay and straw from the farmers, giving them a set income alongside the workforce to harvest it, as this was another of the more localized unit's jobs.

The men from the units were frequently billeted at the farms where they were working, and this was the case on the farm where Elsie Wilkinson lived. Her daughter, Nancy Tipton, took great care to write down her mother's recollections. Taken from Nancy's book of hand written memories is the following:

> One of the many duties the Army had to do during the War was to purchase hay and straw off farms to feed and bed their horses. Sergeant Clifford Montague Felix Beavan, nicknamed Harry for short, was involved in this kind of work.
>
> He was in the RASC (Royal Army Service Corps) and at one time he was billeted, with his mate, at Elm Farm, Spanby, near Sleaford. Their bedroom was up the back stairs, and they would stay at the farm for as long as they needed, until the work in the immediate area had been finished.
>
> Harry drove the baler, which baled the hay up. After the harvest, the Army would buy the hay and straw and then send in some of their men to bale it and transport it. There was a railway station at Aswarby (long since gone now) and some of the hay would be taken there to be sent on by rail. Once they had finished their job, the men would then move on to the other farms where they would do the same.
>
> At Elm Farm though, things were slightly different from the other

jobs. Harry and the farmer's daughter, Elsie Irene Wilkinson, became very good friends. Harry's home was at Fairview, Ocle Pychard, Herefordshire. It was a detached cottage next to Morris's Farm. The friendship between the two progressed, and Elsie went to visit Harry and his family.

Not many people had transport in those days, so when Elsie wanted to visit Harry's family, her father took them to Aswarby Station in the horse and cart, to catch the train to Hereford, where Mr Morris would meet them at the station in the pony and trap, and take them to Harry's home. It was here that Elsie tasted cider for the first time and thought it positively horrible!

Oddly enough, before joining the Army, Harry had done seven years apprenticeship at Claytons and Shuttleworth in Lincoln.

When the Army moved on, Harry used to pushbike from the closer villages where he was billeted to see Elsie. He was five years older than she was, but they were very fond of each other and whenever he went somewhere, he would buy crested china ornaments for her, which she kept safely over the years until her death, aged 104, in 2004, and are still in the family's possession today, a mark of how much she thought of Harry.

Harry survived the Great War and returned home, however the friendship between Elsie and Harry came to a natural end as they slowly lost contact, and Elsie went on to marry a local man and have a family.

Aircraft production in Lincoln

To locals and visitors alike, it may seem difficult to envisage large-scale aircraft production taking place in Lincoln, however this was the case during the Great War, with over 3,500 aircraft flying out of Lincoln, or to put it another way, one in four British aircraft were built in Lincoln.

Sited on West Common in Lincoln, where the former racecourse and grandstand is now to be found, was the airfield for Number 4 Aircraft Acceptance Park. Many of the aircraft were built in the city, taken in large sections and assembled here prior to test flight, and if that was acceptable, they were then flown on to the various squadrons that required replacement aircraft. It was not an uncommon sight for the people of Lincoln to see aircraft being towed to the airfield. In what used to be the Grandstand, overlooking the racecourse, is a mural celebrating the former airfield and the aviation history of the city.

There were three companies in and around Lincoln that were primarily involved in aircraft building:

Clayton & Shuttleworth

The company had been formed in 1842 when Nathaniel Clayton joined with his brother-in-law, Joseph Shuttleworth, and was initially involved in the design and building of agricultural machinery such as steam driven threshing machines. They moved with the times, developing their own engines, and introduced the first combine harvester.

By the beginning of the Great War they were expanding their interests, and by 1916, were making parts for the Submarine Scout Airship. With a foot in the Admiralty's door, it was not long before they had completely turned the factory over to aircraft manufacture, with the first Sopwith Triplane being delivered on 2 December 1916. It is interesting to note that prisoners of war were brought in to help erect Clayton's new aircraft factory. The prisoners were not required to help manufacture aircraft, or weapons, that would actively be used against their countrymen, however it was acceptable for them to be required to erect a building irrespective of its future use.

Only forty-nine of these were made and delivered before they received a new contract in March 1917, this time to build the popular Sopwith Camel, and this aircraft remained in production until the end of the war.

Sopwith Camel. With thanks to **Aeroplane Monthly**

In the meantime, having built new premises specifically for the project, the company began production of another aircraft; this time the Admiralty's contract was for the new Handley Page 0/400 bomber, the largest aircraft being built in the country at the time.

The company, as the others in the city, employed many women in the factories as a matter of necessity. With the amount of work required, and the number of men of working age that were at the Front, the companies had to find a solution to the lack of manpower and they were no doubt pleased that the women could work just as satisfactorily as the men.

Ruston, Proctor & Co

Proctor and Burton was the original name of the company when it began in 1840, becoming known as Ruston, Proctor & Co in 1857, after Joseph Ruston invested in the company.

The company began life specializing in tank locomotives and tank cranes, and kept up with the evolving development in engines and the design and manufacture of tractors, and other agricultural vehicles.

The company was given a contract by the Admiralty to build Sopwith Camels at the beginning of the Great War and went on to build over 2,750 of them and 3000 engines. The aircraft they built also included the Sopwith 1½ Strutters and Royal Aircraft Factory B.E.2s, which were a single-engined, two-seater reconnaissance and light bomber aircraft. A B.E.2 from the Ruston factory was one of the first to shoot down a Zeppelin over England.

The company also produced ammunition, guns, bombs and parts, and built the largest bomb to be made during the Great War. With so many factories in Lincoln making aircraft, ammunition, engines, and other such items that were directly linked to the war effort, the civilian population of the city and surrounding area were able to work and receive a wage whilst feeling that they were 'doing their bit' and contributing to the war effort. No doubt, to many it became personal, as more and more Lincolnshire lads lost their lives overseas.

With so many work places, formerly occupied by men, being available and open to women, there were many poorer families who actually welcomed the event of war, as it provided more jobs and especially openings to women, and would have raised the level of income some of the poorer households in the city.

Marshall, Sons & Co

The company was founded in 1848 and was based on the outskirts of Gainsborough, only a few miles from the city of Lincoln. Initially, the company specialized in steam engines and agricultural vehicles, however, as the hostilities overseas began to pick up pace, the company managed to secure a contract to deliver the Bristol F2B fighter aircraft.

New premises were required, and additional staff, which once again, benefitted the local families, and by the end of the war the company had built 150 of the aircraft, each one being part-assembled and then towed to the airfield on West Common, Lincoln, before being assembled and flight tested.

Robey and Co

King George V and Queen Mary visiting the Robey factory. © Lincs to the Past, Lincs County Council

In 1854, Robert Robey established the company after serving an apprenticeship with Clayton and Shuttleworth. The company, like the others, specialized in design, development and manufacture of agricultural machinery.

Following the lead of the other companies in the city, the company went on to secure an Admiralty contract to build seaplanes, and also the Vickers F.B.5, known as the 'Gunbus', a two-seater fighter aircraft specifically designed for air-to-air combat.

Many of the aircraft that flew out of Lincoln to their new Squadrons sported a unique marking, that of a winged imp. The imp of course, represented the Lincoln Imp as seen on the Cathedral itself. Many flying imps left West Common, all bound for a common mission, and were no doubt recognized by anybody who came from Lincolnshire.

Feeding the nation

When war was first declared, there was a national panic, and shelves in shops nationwide were rapidly cleared as people began to hoard food. Thankfully, there was still a plentiful supply of food across the country for quite some time. The Germans did target some merchant ships, and these were often sunk using submarines. However, it was not until 1916 that food began to become hard to source, and harder still, when in 1917, the Germans began a diligent campaign to starve the British into submission by endeavouring to sink all merchant ships trying to come into the country.

The government had to think of a plan that would ensure the country and its people would stay healthy and therefore productive, despite any restrictions to diet. It was therefore decided that a campaign should begin to encourage people to grow their own food as much as possible, and to encourage landowners, be they large or small, to turn whatever pasture that was not being used for livestock, and surplus land, over to growing produce.

Advertisement and flyers went out across the country encouraging everyone to 'do their bit' and to cultivate every bit of spare land in order to grow vegetables or fruit, or even to keep livestock such as chickens, or perhaps a pig.

In Lincolnshire, as in most households across the country, it was almost a tradition that the man of the house would see to the vegetable plot and the lady of the house have a flower garden, especially to the front of the house, with a small lawn kept with pride. The government was now suggesting that flowers would not sustain a family and that they should be replaced by something more useful. Flower borders were dug up and replanted with potatoes, carrots and other such essentials; those well-kept lawns were dug over and a variety of vegetables planted.

Anyone with a larger garden would have two or three chickens and a cockerel at the end of the garden, which would not only provide a ready supply of eggs, but a hen allowed to brood her eggs could bring off as many as eight to ten chicks, which could be fattened up for the pot, or sold off as 'layers' to other people. Chickens did not need a great deal of looking after and were not expensive to keep, as they would thrive on kitchen scraps.

Pigs were kept in larger gardens, many being housed in homemade sties. Once again, these were not expensive to keep, as all kitchen scraps were fed to the pig. In some villages and towns, a street may have clubbed together in order to build a sty in the garden of one person, and buy a piglet to fatten up. All the houses would put their scraps to one side, and they would be collected and fed to the pig. Once fattened up, the pig would be killed by someone used to doing the job, and butchered into the usual cuts of meat, which would then be shared along the street. The process would then start again.

In a more rural community, with farms scattered across miles, the farmers would share their good fortune with their neighbours; if a pig was killed, then some of the meat would be sent across to nearby neighbouring farms and the favour returned when that farm butchered their own pig.

The old fashioned bartering system came back into fashion, where one person would swap some spare potatoes for some carrots, or some spare eggs for a cauliflower. Farmers with dairy cattle always had extra milk, butter and cheese, and these were exchanged for other goods, or given to friends who were struggling to make ends meet. It was the good old English spirit; all working for a common cause, or should that be all working *against* a common enemy?

On a larger scale, the farmers were encouraged to use up every piece of land possible. Many of the larger farms had, until the war began, large stables with riding ponies and hunters, as well as heavy horses that worked the land. Many of the horses would be commandeered by the Army Remount Service; however, until the call came out to convert as much pasture as possible, some of the farmers still kept their meadows and grazing lands intact. It fast became almost a sin to keep any land with flower gardens and pasture that was unnecessary, and many harsh words were passed between neighbours and the authorities.

It seemed that where possible, every inch of land was being used, even the ground between and besides the huts at the 4th Northern General Hospital in Lincoln was turned over to vegetable patches, and some of the men who were recovering well were encouraged to tend the garden patches by way of occupational therapy. Every little bit helped stated the Government, and it was taken to heart.

Lincolnshire, of course, was a rural county and had always provided a large percentage of the country's vegetables, with potatoes, sugar beet, wheat and barley being some of the staples grown around the county. Transportation of vegetables was helped on some of the farms by what were known as the Potato Railways. These were small gauge railway systems that were set up around some of the larger farms, and would help with ease of transportation from fields to holding yards at the farms, and then onto either main roads or main railway stations.

It was not only potatoes that were transported using these railways, but all of the vegetables harvested on the farm, as well as manure, seeds, etc., back out to the fields. Speed was often essential when harvesting and then transporting vegetables with a shorter lifespan, especially when the produce had to travel many miles to southern counties before actually going on sale.

Small locomotives were used to pull the wagons, and some of the farms employed their own engineers specifically to maintain and work the railways. Similar small gauge railway systems were used on the Western Front to transport supplies to and from the Front Line, and also to transport the wounded to hospital stations further back. After the end of the Great War, many of the wagons and ambulance cars were brought back to England and sold to some of the farms that were still using these small railway systems.

As production on the farms increased, so did the amount of labour required to tend to all the tasks accompanying the successful raising of bountiful crops. Many of the farms still relied on the use of horses, and those were much depleted across the county thanks to the Army requisitioning the horses and leaving the bare minimum needed by the farm to ensure its survival.

With the lack of modern equipment, tasks such as the removal of large stones from pasture land that was being turned over to arable, would have had to be done by hand, with a small cart, either hand or pony driven, being used to transport the picked stones. All this took time; time that the seasons did not allow when manpower was short. Women were now working the land, and in some places, prisoners of war were also adding to the labour force where necessary. However, there was also another source of labour, one that necessity would use.

Children of farming families, especially the poorer families, had long been used as labour on the land. However, as more schools had opened, offering access to education for the poorer families, and to girls as well as boys, children were encouraged to attend school rather than stay at home and help out. With the lack of manpower available however, a rethink was necessary and it was not uncommon for the local, rural schools to allow the children to take time off during certain times of the year when their help was needed on the farms. The potato harvest, and the wheat and barley harvest times were the hardest for the farmers and certainly the boys, and where necessary the older girls of the school would be released for work. One way or another, the crops had to be brought in before inclement weather spoilt the chances of a good harvest.

Older boys in rural counties were also allowed to leave school earlier than the specified age in order to help out on the farms. This was only allowed if they took, and passed, an exit exam showing that they had a basic academic education.

The Labour Corps

There were many people who were classed as unfit for active duty, even though they were keen to do their part. Those who had been serving on the Front Line and were injured and then downgraded as unfit for active service, were also often frustrated, as they wanted to go back to serving their country alongside their friends and family.

There was however, a way for these men to be part of the war effort, and that was to join the Labour Corps. Wives and mothers were often overwhelmed with anger at their spouses and sons; having just been given a chance to avoid the major conflict, they could not understand why their men would want to join the Labour Corps, and more than likely, be posted overseas again.

For some, it was a way to be part of the action, to be able to wear a uniform that you were proud of. Being found unfit for duty, or invalided out of your battalion, did not mean that you wore a placard around your neck declaring for all to see the reason why you were not in uniform, and most unfairly, the men of serving age who were not in uniform were frequently targeted by men and women who believed that they were shirking their duty.

Unfortunately for those joining the Labour Corps, just because they were unfit or wounded and could not serve in an active capacity, did not mean that they would not be working directly on the Front Line and under enemy fire. The Labour Corps personnel were responsible for tasks such as maintaining roads, setting up and maintaining lines of communication, guarding prisoners of war, digging trenches and other jobs that would take the 'active' soldiers away from their duties.

It is interesting to note that men in the Labour Corps could spend prolonged amounts of time actually under enemy fire. In fact, in some cases, they could work under direct enemy fire for longer than the soldiers on active service. So in many cases it was a false scenario that some of the men were offering to their families back home. Telling them that they were 'only in the Labour Corps' and that there was to be 'no active fighting' may have put minds at ease, however the men were well prepared for the reality, and the amount of medals won by the men serving under dire conditions to maintain vital resources for the Armed Forces, serves as a reminder of the men's bravery.

As the Great War progressed and losses increased, joining the Labour Corps also became a matter of conscription. For those men who were deemed unfit for 'normal' duty, they would be categorized according to ability and then placed into one of the Corp's units. Men who were able to walk comfortably for five miles and who were strong and fit, would be put into a Labour Corps attached to a regiment. The Lincolnshire Regiment had their own Labour Corps, and both local men, and men from other regiments who had been wounded and their fitness status downgraded, would be brought together to perform their vital roles.

Men who were not quite as able, and yet relatively fit, would still be able to be enlisted into the Labour Corps, however, they would be employed in work vital to the war effort in this country. Home Service Labour Companies was the name finally settled upon for those units working on home ground.

In Lincolnshire, the obvious use for the Home Service Labour Companies was in the agricultural arena. The farmers were endeavouring to produce as much food as possible to compensate for the loss of food coming in from overseas, and with the amount of men serving overseas, manpower on the fields was lacking. The Land Army women worked hard and accounted for some of the loss of manpower, as did the extra help from PoWs. However, the men from the Home Service Labour Companies certainly helped production by adding their manpower where necessary. Smaller units were scattered across the county, and the men sent out from these on a daily basis. Any increase in manpower, no matter where it was procured from, was a bonus for those struggling from the loss of manpower due to enlistment.

The Labour Corps, in its various forms, eventually had over 389,900 men on active service. Just over 175,000 were recruited into the Home Service Labour Companies and worked 'at home', and although most were to be posted many miles from their actual home, there was still the consolation that at least they were not on the Front Line, were not risking life and limb, and they were also doing their bit for the war effort and would not be condemned as shirkers or cowards.

CHAPTER FOUR

1916/17 – Seeing It Through

As the New Year dawned, there was no change to the conflict overseas or the conditions for the families back home. More women were stepping up to take the place of the men in agriculture and industry in order to keep production flowing. The government needed to find more ways to increase manpower in order to increase production and keep the country running as smoothly as possible, and so another source of workers had to be found.

Prisoners of War

It was inevitable that there would be prisoners taken during the course of the Great War, however, even before the conflict had truly begun, the Government had to make provision for those people of foreign descent that may have been sympathetic to the German cause. These 'aliens' were interned for the duration of the conflict, sometimes in purpose built camps and often in farms, where they could add to the manpower and do a useful job.

As the fighting progressed along the Front Line, there began to be a logistical problem with the amount of prisoners that were being taken. It simply was not practical to build long-term camps for these prisoners of war, as that would take manpower and also mean that in the event of a riot and possible breakout, the British would be caught between the enemy in front of them and a possible enemy force consisting of prisoners advancing from behind. As the majority of PoWs were captured in whole units rather than the odd soldier here and there, a breakout would have been a much larger threat. The solution was to transport the prisoners back to Britain and hold them there for the duration of the war.

Prisoner of war camps were scattered across the country, not only to ensure that the men were not within easy walking distance of each other, but in order to make use of them rather than simply hold them safely. It seemed sensible to give the men some sort of work to do; if left to their own devices, mischief could have been planned, and the merits of adding to the national work force, as well as giving these men a constructive occupation, seemed to be a winning formula.

The prisoners were assessed to see whether they had any skills that could be of use. There was no value in sending a former quarry worker to work a plough, whilst his friend who was a farmer, went to work in the quarry! The men were keen to work, to have some form of occupation to make the days pass quickly, and this was not to be slave labour; those who 'employed' the PoWs had to give them a minimum wage, out of which a percentage would be taken towards their keep, and the rest was for them. The men were not to be employed in any form of industry that was linked to war work. This of course, was for practical reasons as well as ethical, as it would not have been right to make the men operate machinery that was making bullets to kill their fellow countrymen, and there would have been the risk of sabotage had they been put into this position.

Men would be sent out from the larger camps, or smaller, working parties would be boarded closer to their work. Lincolnshire's PoWs and internee workers were to be found in the following places:

> *Boston Docks, civilian working party.*
> *Bracebridge Agricultural Depot, Bracebridge, Lincoln.*
> *Burton Hall Agricultural Group, Burton Hall, Lincoln.*
> *Folkingham Agricultural Group, attached to Sleaford.*
> *Grantham Working Camp, Belton Park.*
> *Great Hale Agricultural Group, Great Hale, Heckington.*
> *Gringley-on-the-Hill Agricultural Group, Gainsborough.*
> *Hogsthorpe Agricultural Group.*
> *Holbeach Agricultural Group.*
> *Morton Agricultural Group.*
> *Nocton Agricultural Group.*

Partney Agricultural Group.
Pinchbeck Road Agricultural Group.
Sleaford Working Camp.
Somerby Hall Agricultural Group.
Spalding Group.
Stainby Working Group.
Stow Park Agricultural Group.
Timberland Agricultural Group.
Wainfleet Agricultural Group.
Wingland Working Camp.
Witham Agricultural Group.

As you can see from the above list, there were many groups of PoWs working on the land in Lincolnshire. It is interesting to see the changing times that saw women, and what were to the locals 'foreigners', working together on the farms. It must be remembered that at this period in history, the more rural counties such as Lincolnshire, would not have had much contact with people from other countries. The small communities were very self-contained and introverted, supporting each other with fierce allegiance, but with a strong suspicion of 'outsiders', even those who were English, but from a different village or town. It was difficult for the people, and those they had to work alongside, to cope with the language barrier and the knowledge that these men had been fighting 'our boys', as well as the fact that they were simply not from 'round here'.

In the beginning, the men were kept at a distance from the English workers on the farm, be that women or men. However, as it became more apparent that the prisoners had no intention of escaping and were happy to turn their hands to honest work in return for a wage, and to eat as well as those on the farm, the security around them lapsed somewhat. In some areas the men were trustees, and slowly, friendships began to blossom between those working side by side on a daily basis.

This was not always a good thing; although natural for a couple that was coming into contact with each other on a daily basis to begin to forge a deeper relationship, especially considering the lack of men to socialize with outside work hours, the circumstances that brought them together would also endeavour to keep them apart. There was of course, bad will against the PoWs, and for those women who began romantic relationships with them, the local community were not beyond ostracizing them.

Lincolnshire was a county of small, rural villages and, in many cases, simply a group of houses that were the estate worker's houses. Such small, introverted communities took things to heart. The loss of a husband, father or brother would be keenly felt in such a small place where others may have been lost also, and despite the PoWs no longer taking part in hostilities, grudges were held towards them as they were seen as the ones holding the gun when an Englishman died. With this in mind it was inconceivable for an English girl to 'betray' her countrymen by becoming friendly with one of the 'hun'.

There was rough treatment for these girls; it was not uncommon for them to be jeered, spat at and cursed as they walked along. In some cases, the girl was moved from the farm or the PoW was removed, however, it did not always deter the relationship, a fact borne out by the amount of former PoWs who settled in this country post-war, with a similar situation arising during the Second World War.

The prisoners of war provided a great source of manpower on the Lincolnshire farms during the Great War, enabling more land to be turned to food production and providing vital manpower during harvest time, when it was the usual battle between man and the elements to get the harvest in before it was spoilt by the weather; despite there being a war on, the fundamental issues of life did not change.

On the whole, it was felt that those men who were prisoners in Britain and the surrounding islands were treated far better than our own men who had been captured. The Geneva Convention had been agreed upon before the start of hostilities, and the Red Cross had been given relevant permissions to visit the prisoner of war camps on both sides to ensure that conditions were as they should be. Unfortunately, although 'we' considered that the prisoners in British care were well looked after, receiving a fair wage for their circumstances and decent food to eat, the same could not be said for the British prisoners abroad.

There were reports coming back that the food was terrible; very short rations, in some cases perhaps four tiny raw potatoes to last the day. Medical care seemed to be better than the nutritional care, however, there was hope for the men, as the Red Cross were able to bring in food and comfort parcels for them.

In many places, the communities rallied round to raise money or food that they could send across with the Red Cross to their men in the camps. For many of the prisoners, the food parcels meant the difference between life and death, with the men dropping weight very quickly if they were solely dependent on the camp diet.

The Lincolnshire people rallied as best they could, bearing in mind any rationing that was in place in their area. Being a rural community did have its benefits, as some foodstuffs were more available than others. They either donated food items, or money was raised in order to buy in items that could be packed up and sent.

It was another case of 'doing our bit'; in this case the families knew exactly where the food parcels were going and that they would directly help their loved ones to stay well.

It was not just members of the Armed Forces who were in the prisoner of war camps. A number of civilians were also in the camps for a variety of reasons. One such group was trawler men out of Boston Docks, whose ships had been sunk, and they had subsequently been 'rescued' and taken prisoner. The town of Boston rallied round the men, raising funds and food items, and sending a total of 9,100 boxes of food, having raised over £3,000 to cover the cost. In a town with a poor economy, many men away at war, and the fishing trade seriously depleted by loss of boats and men, this was no mean feat, and showed the determination of the community to rally round their men, even if they were not immediately related to them.

High cost to families

1917 began with no sign of hostilities ceasing. People in the local communities still ended their days praying for loved ones overseas and began the following day wondering whether they had survived the night, and all the accompanying horrors that that brought.

For one woman in particular, each day must have been a struggle, worrying for the safety of her sons. Amy Beechey, of Avondale Street, Lincoln, had lost her husband, the former Vicar of Friesthorpe in 1912 to cancer, and her sons had heeded the call to volunteer as eagerly as other local lads.

Even her sons Chris and Harold, who had emigrated to Australia,

Gravestone of Amy Beechey, who lost five sons during the First World War.

joined the Australian Imperial Force after their farming endeavours were struck by drought and failure.

The first son to join up was Barnard, Bar, the eldest of the family, who joined the Army almost as soon as war was declared. At this point there was talk of the war ending before Christmas, and families were proud of their sons, waving off the lines of volunteers as they marched the best that they could, out of the city to the waiting transport that would take them off to basic training camps. Over the course of the next few months, Amy watched as each of her sons joined various regiments.

Chris and Harold were the first of the brothers to come under direct fire in Gallipoli. The brothers looked out for each other, and Chris wrote home to assure his mother of Harold's well being.

Unfortunately for Chris, a stretcher-bearer, he was not able to continue in his self-appointed role of guardian to Harold, as he was shot whilst on duty, falling into a ravine and temporarily paralysing his legs. Some would say that he was lucky; the role of stretcher-bearer being one that brought great risk to the personnel who went out into some of the most dangerous territory in order to bring back the wounded. He was sent back to Britain to convalesce, where Harold was to join him after contracting a serious case of dysentery. By this point, Amy Beechey would have received two communications from the War Office informing her of the wounding of Chris, and that Harold had contracted dysentery and was recovering. I wonder whether, at this point, she thought that this would be the worst that could befall her family.

All of Amy's children were copious letter writers, regularly writing to reassure her of their well-being, so the absence of letters must have been a forewarning of bad tidings to come. In October 1915, after the Battle of Loos, she received another letter from the War Department. This time the news was devastating; Barnard had been killed in action whilst serving with the Lincolnshire Regiment. Hostilities were picking up pace and with her other sons serving in their respective regiments, and Harold recovering well and on his way to being signed off as fit for duty, it must have been a sombre Christmas and New Year for the Beechey family as they anticipated the coming year with only Chris safe from danger, albeit still recovering from serious injuries, which would eventually prevent him returning to duty.

Contact between the boys and the family was regular, with Amy often sending out 'comfort parcels' to them. Lice powder was frequently requested, and families across the county and Britain, would be sending out packages with little luxuries in, such as hand knitted mittens, socks and balaclavas, chocolate, dry biscuits, soap and shaving cream. Anything that might literally bring a little bit of home comfort to their family members, that would travel and keep well, and that would make the sender feel as if they were doing their bit for the war effort and for their sons, brothers or husbands.

When Harold rejoined his regiment at Pozieres, the Battle of the

Somme had already taken a great toll and he was posted back into the middle of the action. Meanwhile, back home, in a tight knit community, it was becoming evident that the casualties were huge, and it must have been somewhat of a relief when Amy received word from Harold himself, to say that although he had been injured by shrapnel that had passed through his arm and into his chest, that he was alive and away from the action to once again recuperate.

Amy now knew, first hand, the risk of being part of the Battle of the Somme, so the news that Frank was, and that Charlie would soon be, somewhere along those lines, must have worried her terribly. Across the city, bands of women would come together with their worries, knitting needles and the essential pot of tea between them, sympathizing and consoling each other. These were the days where everyone in the street knew each other, where the majority of people had lived in the street for so long that they knew everyone else, had watched their own children grow up alongside their neighbours, and as such, each felt the loss of the other's child as keenly as their own. These groups of women who supported each other through the worry and grief may well have been the modern day equivalent of the self-help group; offering support, comfort and help where necessary.

On 14 November 1916, Frank was caught by a shell burst, which irreparably damaged his legs, leading to his death, and Amy was to receive her first telegram informing her that one of her sons had died. This was not to be the last. Harold was the next to lose his life on 10 April 1917, when he was killed by a shell blast in Arras. It seemed a sad turn of events, considering his two previous injuries that had not been severe enough to invalid him out of the Army.

Having lost two sons already, Amy dreaded the sight of the telegram boy, and although her remaining sons were regularly in contact with her, she must have experienced some trepidation when seeing the postman coming up the road. Throughout Lincoln and the surrounding villages, women wrestled on a daily basis, with the guilt that came with the overwhelming sense of relief as the telegram boy knocked on the door of the house across the road, or when they read in the casualty lists that their son was safe.

In October, Amy was not to be so lucky and it was her turn, once again, to receive news that Char had lost his life whilst attempting an ammunition run in Tanzania.

Len was understandably concerned about his mother and upset over the loss of his brothers. Perhaps he felt that the odds were now in his favour; that surely no family could be so unlucky as to lose so many members of the family, or perhaps he knew the reality of the situation and wondered when his time would come.

Unfortunately, Len was to join his brothers in December 1917. Struggling with illness already, the Battle of Cambrai, on 30 November 1917, left him wounded and suffering with gas poisoning. Despite all efforts, he contracted tetanus, and once again the Beechy family had a dreary start to the New Year.

Amy spent 1918 fretting over the health and well-being of Eric, and worrying about the imminent departure of Sam who was to join up in the October. Thankfully, the hostilities ended soon after and Amy was to reflect on the last few years; the loss of five of her sons, and the serious wounding of Chris. Prayers of thanks were offered up for the safe return of Eric and Sam.

Prior to her death, Amy requested to be buried near the graves of soldiers, as all of her boys who had died were buried overseas and she had not been able to visit any of their graves. She felt the need to be close to those who had paid the ultimate sacrifice, just like her own boys. As with all the families who had lost men in the conflict, they were never far from her thoughts over the subsequent years.

Sergeant John William Warrener

Across the county there were similar stories, although no one family lost as many sons as Amy Beechy. However, there were other stories just a poignant. Take, for example, Sergeant John William Warrener of the 14 Brigade, Australian Field Artillery unit.

Sergeant Warrener's father had emigrated to Australia, living in Yangan, Queensland, but his father was a Lincolnshire 'yellow belly'. John had never met his English family, just read letters and heard the stories of the rural upbringing on what was his grandparent's small farm. Once his unit had arrived in England and he was given leave, he arranged to visit the family.

It was a joyous visit; many tales were told of family life in Australia and great delight was taken in telling stories about his father, Samuel's, youth. It was a bittersweet gift, brought about by the event of the War. If John had not enlisted in Australia, then he would never have had an opportunity to meet his family in England. No doubt there were many similar visits taking place across the country.

At the end of his visit, just as he was leaving, he reached to his cap and pulled out one of the feathers and gave it to his cousin as a keepsake. That feather must have taken on a great significance when the news came that he had lost his life on 18 October 1917. At the age of 22, Sergeant John Warrener was buried in Etaples Military Cemetery, France, grave reference XXX.E 8.

On 14 April 2000, Nancy Tipton, daughter of John's cousin, made the trip to Etaples Cemetery on behalf of the family, to find his grave and lay a wreath of remembrance. On his grave is the inscription, '*It was a noble sacrifice, a glorious end. The Lord's will be done.*'

War work for women

With a high percentage of the male work force overseas, there began to be problems in the factories and on the land, where the main work force were predominantly male. It should be remembered that at this point in history, women were generally expected to remain in the home once married, and women in paid occupations were in office work, nursing and similar. It was simply unheard of for women to do the same work as men; they truly were considered the gentler sex and perhaps not expected to be as able as the men.

By the time conscription had begun in earnest, it was evident that the country was beginning to struggle in many industries. Lincolnshire was predominantly a farming county and the farms were beginning to struggle due to lack of farmhands. In 1915, the Board of Agriculture set up the Women's Land Army, and sent out officials to persuade those farmers who were not happy to employ women to work on their land.

By the end of 1917 it was estimated that there were over 250,000 working as farm labourers across the country, not all of those members of the WLA. Women were expected to work 50 hours in the summer and forty-eight hours in the winter, however, in reality, the women worked as long as was necessary and were expected to do every task that a male labourer would have done; ploughing, threshing, milking, feeding, etc.

Accommodation was generally provided by the farmer, as were the wages, and conditions varied from farm to farm, as did the wages, dependent on how much the farmer would charge for accommodation and food.

In 1919 the WLA was disbanded, leaving many women unemployed in order make way for the men who were returning to work. The Women's Land Army was to be reformed at the beginning of the Second World War, where it again played a vital role in feeding the country.

Zeppelin shot down over coast

The airships had been causing great consternation across the countryside, and whether by design, poor navigational skills or adverse weather conditions, Lincoln and the county itself had appeared to have been targeted by these silent monsters.

There was one particular event during this year, which demonstrated the ill feeling towards the Zeppelins and their crews. Our defences had successfully shot down a Zeppelin, which came down into the sea off the Lincolnshire coast, and William Martin, Captain of the trawler King

Stephen, based in Grimsby, saw distress signals whilst out at sea and went to investigate, fearing that it was one of our boats in trouble.

As he arrived at the scene, he quickly realized that it was in fact the remains of a Zeppelin and its crew. He took the decision not to attempt a rescue, preferring instead to return to shore and raise the alarm there, which would enable Naval boats to attend the scene.

His unwillingness to attempt a rescue was criticized and supported in equal measures. In his defence, William Martin said that the Germans were armed, and outnumbered his own crew, and he believed that they would be safe enough until a rescue was effected by armed Naval personnel. These were difficult times indeed, however, the incident was well reported and boosted morale across the country, especially in those areas frequently targeted by Zeppelins.

Raising much needed funds – the Tank Banks

Lincoln was to be at the forefront of raising much needed funds towards the war effort, thanks to the pioneering invention of the tank. Initially, the civilian workers, male and female, considered their role in tank production as helping to build a machine that would help in the Front Line battles overseas, thus saving lives and hopefully shortening the war. Nobody realized just how popular the tank was to become and how the public took the vehicle to heart.

In November 1917, a tank took part in the Lord Mayor's Show in London. The public was enamoured of the machines, having kept abreast of the battles and the success stories that included the tanks. As far as the public was concerned, anything that could wreak havoc on the 'hun' and help to keep 'our boys' safe was no bad thing.

The government was looking for a way to raise revenue and to increase interest in the War Bonds and War Savings Certificates. They were quick to seize on the idea to link the fund raising with the popularity of the tanks.

The plan was to use a number of tanks and to take them across the country, stopping at the major towns and cities along the way. Once in the town, a table would be set up inside the tank, and the people would take turns to come up and hand over their money through an opening. One of the first tanks, 141 Egbert, was brought back from France and still bore the battle scars. This tank was the most popular as it had taken an active role in the fighting, and so another twist to the campaign was launched; whichever place managed to raise the most money would be given Egbert to place on permanent display in the town. The campaign captured people's imagination and they began to save money, ready for when one of the tanks visited their area.

There were six tanks that toured across the country; 113 Julian, 119 Old Bill, 130 Nelson, 137 Drake, 141 Egbert and 142 Iron Ration. People travelled from villages nearby to the larger town or cities, with hundreds gathering to see the tank visiting their area. The visit was made into an occasion, with troops accompanying the tank, sometimes a flypast, and support from dignitaries and politicians; anything and everything that could be thought of and done to elevate the occasion, heighten interest and excitement, which in turn would, hopefully, increase revenue.

Lincoln held a week of celebrations and fund-raising in March 1918. The tank itself was situated on the Cornhill, and with the railway giving ready access into the city, Lincoln was flooded with supporters, most with money in their pockets. It seemed that the people of Lincoln only had one focus during the years between 1914 and 1918, and that was the war effort. Not only were the factories turning out tanks, aircraft and ammunitions, with the employees tirelessly working to keep production up, there were the airfields operating locally and across Lincolnshire. And then there were the fundraising efforts that had been going on throughout the war years. Those who did not have enough money to pay for a War Bond or Savings Certificate would often donate what they had towards the fund. Once again, it was a way for the public to feel that they were physically helping those fighting abroad.

Over the course of the Tank Bank campaign, over £2,000,000 was raised, with West Hartlepool winning Tank Egbert after raising a total of £2,367,333, and Egbert was given pride of place in the town. In 1919, many of the other towns and cities that had raised large amounts of money for the war effort were given tanks that had served at the Front by way of thanks. Although these have long since gone, there remains one in Ashford, Kent, which, due to having an electricity substation sited within the body of the tank, was not able to be removed, and is now preserved as an official war memorial.

The Museum of Lincolnshire Life, Lincoln, has on display one of the smaller tanks, named 'Flirt', a timely reminder of one of the city's contributions to the war effort and, not to be forgotten, the tanks that were designed and manufactured in Lincoln all those years ago were the forerunners of those designed and used today.

CHAPTER FIVE

1918 – The Final Blows

The beginning of 1918 and we were still at war. The country's morale was low, with no visible end to the conflict or the struggles that faced the communities at home. Food stores were as low as morale; it seemed that there was little to look forward to.

The King and Queen visit Lincolnshire.

Tuesday, 9 April 1918, dawned with a buzz of excitement across Lincoln. King George V and the Queen were due to visit the county, beginning in Lincoln, in order to recognize the contribution that the city, its people and surrounding area, had made to the war effort.

The city's station and all areas of the visit had been cleaned and smartened up as best it could be, in readiness for the important visitors. This was to be a massive boost to Lincoln, her residents and also for those wounded in action who were still in the city's hospitals and convalescent homes.

The train pulled into the station at ten o'clock and the King was greeted and welcomed by the Mayor and Mayoress, Lincoln's Sheriff, other dignitaries, and then treated to a welcome from schoolchildren waiting in the station. The war may still have been going on, but greeting the King and Queen was an important event in anybody's life, and the children's mothers had done their best to turn out their offspring in their best clothes, whether they were made from 'hand me downs', an outfit borrowed for the day, or a dress, for example, that had been made from something else, such as an adult's dress cut down. Pride was uppermost in everyone's thoughts, pride in country, the serving forces, the Royal Family and in themselves.

The children were not the only ones providing a welcome for the visitors. As well as the crowds that had gathered along the route they would take, there was also a large contingency of the Lincolnshire Regiment who were turned out in uniforms, with boots and buckles shining in the best Army tradition.

The initial purpose of the visit was to visit the city's factories. Without these factories, and the initial designing of the tanks, the outcome of the war could have been very different. King George V felt it his duty to personally thank the workers involved in the respective projects, and to the delight of those involved in the manufacture of the tanks, he asked to take a ride in one of them. What a thrill for the workers to see their King so enthused by one of their tanks in the first place, but watching him ride in one would have brought home to them exactly how much their work had meant towards the war effort.

Other factories such as Robeys and Clayton, and Shuttleworth were also visited. Lincoln offered such a variety of equipment that was deemed vital for the war effort, such as ammunitions, tanks and aircraft, that the King and Queen had quite an itinerary to fulfil in order to visit every factory in the city to offer thanks and support. The King was, as most men were and still are, most interested in the tanks, aircraft and ammunition production, thoroughly enjoying seeing the finished articles.

By the time of the Royal visit, many of the factories were staffed by more women workers than men; a fact that must have been reflected in other visits across the country similar to the one to Lincoln. In many of the factories the King awarded medals to the workers, congratulating them on their hard work and dedication to 'the cause'.

Whilst in Lincoln, the King and Queen were presented to Amy Beechy, who had been invited to meet the couple, as she was the ideal representation of all the women in Lincoln who had lost sons and loved ones during the conflict. Amy had been identified as the mother who had lost the most sons during the conflict, and thanks to this dubious honour, she was introduced to the Royal couple. It was here that the Queen was able to find common ground, compassion and understanding. Amy was thanked for her great sacrifice to which she replied, '*It was no sacrifice, Ma'am, I did not give them willingly.*' Those dignitaries surrounding the King and Queen may well have been horrified at the audacity of her reply, however, another mother would easily have understood her heartfelt words and the emotion behind them. An honour indeed to be introduced to the couple, however, I'm sure Amy would have gladly taken her place amongst the crowds waving at the visitors, in the sure knowledge that at least one more of her sons was safe.

The next visit was to the 4th Northern General Hospital, to offer appreciation to the staff for their dedication to duty, and also to see the wounded soldiers. Whilst at the hospital, King George awarded medals to fourteen soldiers. If deemed fit, these soldiers would find themselves back on the Front as soon as possible, but this time with a story to tell, which would while away the long hours and bring some light from home into the dreary trenches.

A visit to the city of Lincoln would not be complete without calling in at the Cathedral. The standard of the Lincolnshire Regiment was presented and the couple took part in prayers, remembering those of the Regiment fighting overseas. The people of Lincoln were grateful to see their sovereigns honouring the city, the factories, workers, the injured, those caring for them, and remembering the lost, wounded and still serving, in prayers. The visit unified the city and the county; even those that were not able to get into the city, or close to the other parts of the county that were visited, still knew that the visit was in progress, and the visit was a morale booster for everyone.

The following day, the couple arrived at Immingham to celebrate all things naval, and were greeted by a Naval Guard of honour. The couple also had the opportunity to meet the newer, female ranks of the service. On this occasion, the King had over fifty men to present medals to, including the local minesweepers. As on the previous day, the Royal couple made time to visit a church for prayer, this time using the Naval Church of St Nicholas. More visits to engineering works took place, with the King showing his enthusiasm for the different processes.

In the afternoon, the couple went on to Grimsby, where they were shown around the town by the Lord and Lady Mayoress. On this occasion, the planned visit was slightly different, because not only did they visit the shell factory on Victoria Street, but they also visited the fish curing factory, and were taken through the curing process. Once again, it was noticeable that the staff was mainly women.

The visit to Lincolnshire was concluded on the 11 April by a visit to Cranwell to inspect the newly formed Royal Air Force station. Prince Albert met the couple, and no doubt, was thrilled to show the King around and into a Handley-Page aircraft. The King had enjoyed the visit to the area and his taste of tanks, aircraft and munitions that were being produced by the men and women of Lincolnshire.

Rationing Introduced

By 1918, food shortages had begun to take their toll. The Government had tried to control food consumption by increasing the cost of certain food staples, however, it became evident that in some parts of the country the poorer families were beginning to suffer from malnutrition. The campaign to encourage people to grow their own food was only effective for families that had the facilities to do this; those in flats or with little garden, simply did not have the resources at hand.

After much discussion, the Government realized that there was no option but to introduce rationing, and this was put into place at the beginning of 1918, with sugar being one of the very first food items to be put on ration. Everyone was issued with a ration book, which showed the entitlements for each week. Butter, margarine, meat and other commodities were slowly added to the items on the ration cards, and each person had to be registered at a specific shop, and use that one shop to acquire their provisions.

Food was not the only thing to be rationed. Towards the end of the Great War, coal was also put on ration, and scavenging for wood to supplement the coal ration was the only way to make your ration stretch, especially when the weather was so cold.

It was not unusual to see long queues of housewives waiting their turn outside the grocers, butchers or bakers. Those more affluent households would send one of their servants to stand in line and collect the rations, but for others, standing in line and waiting at the various shops could, and often did, take up the majority of the day.

Bread was eventually rationed too, and was sold by the weight, not by the loaf. Smaller pieces of bread, similar to a bread roll, were made, in order to make up the accurate weight allotted. These small rolls were called makeweights. The bakeries also had to use Government Issued recipes to ensure that everybody was eating the same amount of grain.

Lincolnshire, being such a rural county, fared better than some places. However, this was very much dependent on where a person lived. In the city, families with small terraced houses, in streets such as Ewart Street and Dixon Street, had next to no gardens in which to grow their own vegetables, and so relied solely on the rations and availability in the shops. Some families were lucky enough to have relatives who lived in a more rural setting, and who would travel into the city in order to bring their family extra provisions. However, there were plenty of families who did not, and the lack of food was terribly demoralizing.

Those in the countryside fared better, even if it meant gleaning the odd tiny potato from the fields that may have been missed by those harvesting them. Even the children were clever enough to spot anything that may have fallen off the back of a cart, when being transported, and these occasional finds added to the vegetables that a family would be able to grow themselves. Chickens, pigs and sometimes even an orphan lamb would be kept at the bottom of the garden if it was big enough, and a dairy farm was able to produce extra butter, cheese and milk.

The communities did look after each other; if someone ran out of butter or margarine, then a neighbour would help out where possible. The elderly, infirm and very young were taken care of, and if someone in the street happened to be brought some extra provisions by a friend or relative, then they would often share a little something with their neighbours, knowing that their turn would come.

Lincoln did not escape the black marketeers; there was always someone who was happy to profit from misfortune, and Lincolnshire had its fair share of these unsavoury characters.

The rationing continued after the end of the Great War, as the country needed time to re-establish supply lines and stock levels. So hard was the country hit by food shortages that some items remained on rationing until 1920. The lessons were learnt and when the Second World War began, rationing was implemented much earlier in order to maintain adequate food stocks and nutrition.

Football

It was inevitable that many players did not, or could not, return to their football clubs after the end of the hostilities; there had been so many men lost and wounded that all of the clubs across the country struggled to immediately bring their teams back to the standard that they were at prior to The Great War, and Lincoln City Football Club's manager, Jack Strawson, had to begin the unenviable task of trying to recreate the 'Dream Team' of the 1911/12 season, ready for the resumption of the National League in 1919.

Lincoln City Football Club, their supporters and committee, alongside the country's other football clubs, would stand in remembrance and tribute to those players who had once graced their turf and who were never to return.

Influenza Epidemic

As the men were de-mobbed and returned home, the families rejoiced, grateful that their loved ones had survived the fighting and the conditions overseas. In many cases, the men came home with disabilities or injuries that would impact on their chances of returning to the work that they used to do before joining up. The families were happy to have them home in whatever capacity, just so long as they were alive.

Unfortunately, the optimism that arrived home with the men was, in many cases, short-lived. The men brought home with them a gift, not one to treasure, but one that the people of Lincolnshire, and the country in general, came to dread. Influenza, commonly known as the Spanish Flu, had taken hold of the men and in many cases killed them before they could get as far as home. This disease was not just confined to Britain, it was a worldwide epidemic, and by the time the disease had disappeared, it had claimed the lives of over 50,000,000 people around the world.

With so many men at close quarters, the disease spread quickly, and the poor nutrition and conditions that the men had been fighting in, helped the disease to progress faster, accumulating more victims literally by the minute. Where once the military hospitals were full of wounded men, now the wards began to fill up with those suffering from influenza. As the disease took hold, graves could not be dug fast enough, nor coffins put together quickly enough, and so large holes were dug by machinery and the bodies were buried without coffins.

It was not just the men from the forces who were succumbing to the disease. The men brought it back home with them, and very quickly the disease spread across the country. It was a strange complication of it that took those who were fit and healthy too. It seemed that in a person who was fit, healthy and well fed, the immune system over reacted to the disease, with fatal results. Nobody was immune, and many families went from celebrating the return of a soldier to mourning his passing within a few weeks, and dreading the symptoms that others were then showing.

The 4th Northern General Hospital in Lincoln was slowly beginning to take in more patients suffering from influenza, and the local papers were now reporting on deaths of servicemen generally cited as being from 'pneumonia following influenza.' As more patients were admitted, the staff also began to contract the disease and staffing levels began to suffer, with those healthy enough to work taking on extra shifts, which in turn put them in peril of contracting the disease as they were worn out, taking little care of themselves whilst caring for their patients.

Doctors and nurses across the county were run ragged. In the rural communities, the doctors had many patients spread across the countryside, and once the disease was well established, were physically unable to cope with them all. In some villages there were ladies who served as midwives to the women, who now also took on the role of nurse for the living, and the laying out of the dead. The disease was so bad that there were cases where a family may have lived some distance from the village, and when they were not seen for a while, a distant neighbour would have visited, only to find that the whole family had died, or that perhaps, as in a couple of cases, the parents were dead and the baby was still alive in its cot.

Precautions were taken; schools were closed, and in some parishes there were fewer church services, especially where the vicar or minster had been taken poorly themselves, rather than actually closing the church due to infection risks. The advice given to people was to go

Lincoln War Memorial, located at Saint Benedict's Church.

home to bed if they felt ill, keep warm, eat to keep their strength up, and to call in the doctor when necessary.

In a predominantly rural county, where livestock depended on manpower for feed and care, a farmer would often push through the early signs of influenza in order to do vital jobs on the farm, only to wear himself out and succumb to the disease. There were many wives who rejoiced in having the bread winner return from war, considering their future brighter as the 'man of the house' had returned to care for the family, only to find themselves widowed anyway. Thankfully, the war years had seen industry and farming etc., becoming more open to female workers, and this would be beneficial in the years afterwards when women were obliged to find jobs themselves in order to keep the family solvent, whether that be because their husbands had died on active service, from influenza, or because they had been seriously injured and no longer able to work.

What a cruel twist of fate to end the war, only to present another catastrophe that saw the population of the country seriously affected.

Erecting War Memorials

As the Great War drew to a close, the scale of the losses was realized as a whole. Very few places had avoided losing any members of the community, and there was a countrywide need to express thanks, and mourn the loss of those who had died.

The more affluent families in the county erected their own memorials, generally by way of a plaque in the local Parish Church or Chapel, or even on or around the battlefields where their loved ones lost their lives. There were plaques erected in sports halls, factories, etc., where many men would never return. Every community was determined to have a central memorial where they could gather to remember and commemorate those lost in the line of duty. Fundraising began, local councils trawled through budgets to find money for the memorial, and designing began. In many places, land was acquired, as the memorial itself would be placed in a memorial garden.

There was, however, the odd village scattered across the country where there was no need to stand a memorial. Minting, near Horncastle, was one such place; a small village with under 200 occupants, who proudly supported the 10 men who went off to serve their country. With such a small community, those 10 men would have been sorely missed, and the impact of losing them would have hit hard. Thankfully, all the men returned after the end of the war, and so no memorial was needed. The Parish Church now has a plaque commemorating those men's service, and offering thanks for their safe return.

Over the coming years, the memorials were planned, built and dedicated. However, there were sometimes unforeseen problems that would hold up the erection of a memorial for lengthy periods, generally an issue of funding or placing of the memorial, but none of the memorials were delayed for as long as the one in the village of Fulstow, close to Louth, which was not erected until 2005.

It was a contentious issue that prevented the memorial from being erected, one that divided the village; the best course of action was considered to be to delay putting a memorial into the village, indefinitely. Somewhat harsh perhaps, but the issue was a complicated one.

Seven men died serving their country, however, another of the villagers also lost his life, although he was officially shot for cowardice and desertion. Private Charles Kirman was by no means a coward. He had served in the Army for nine years before resigning, and was happy to join again when the hostilities began, and he was called up. A seasoned soldier, he was not unused to active service and the Army life in general, however the hardship and horrors of serving on the Front Line took its toll in a way he would never have imagined. He was not alone; many suffered in a similar way with what we would now consider to be Post Traumatic Stress Disorder. However, the diagnosis then of shell shock, was not recognized for some time, and was, sadly, not considered as a factor in Private Kirman's case.

Private Kirman fought valiantly at Mons and on the Somme, and was wounded twice, recovering sufficiently to be returned to duty. He had joined up with friends from the village and had watched them being injured, and in some cases watched them die. The horrors of the Front Line, the death and despair, coupled with his own injuries, psychologically damaged him, and unable to face life at the Front, he went AWOL. After a few days he handed himself in, was court-martialled and sent back to the lines, where he panicked and ran again.

Once again he returned, but eventually was deemed a persistent offender and was again court-martialled for cowardice and desertion.

In his defence, he said that he suffered from crippling headaches when at the Front Line, said he did not know what he was doing, and even mentioned that his nerves were damaged. None of this was taken into account, and so Private Kirman was shot at dawn on 23 September 1917.

Back home in Fulstow, a close knit community, the distress was tangible and when a memorial was proposed for the men who had lost their lives in the conflict, it was suggested that Private Kirman should not be added to the list due to his conviction and execution. Some of the village agreed, however, those that had known Charles, especially those whose sons had fought alongside him, and even those who had lost sons, were adamant that they did not want their sons mentioned on the memorial unless the name of Private Kirman was remembered alongside them.

The debate went back and forth over a number of years, and so sensitive was the subject that the village did not even hold services of remembrance. Over the years, the issue slowly dimmed and was forgotten until brought up again, and a successful campaign launched, to finally add a memorial plaque in the Church to remember ALL the men lost during the Great War.

Since the decision to add Private Kirman to the Fulstow memorial, the government made the momentous, and long-campaigned for decision, to give a full pardon to all men who were shot at dawn for cowardice and desertion; over 300 in total. Recognizing that these men were more than likely suffering from a stress-related medical condition at the time, the families of these men were overjoyed at the decision, and across the country the names of these men have been added to memorials.

Living with Shell Shock

Many men returned from the Front with injuries that would affect them for the rest of their lives; amputations, blindness and chest conditions often meant that these men would never be able to hold down a job again, and would rely on their wives working and a disability pension. The families of these men found it relatively easy to adapt to life with their conditions, unlike the families of those men who were suffering from the psychological condition, which came to be known as shell shock, a term that Medical Officer, Charles Myers, first began to use.

The condition presented itself in many ways, triggering physical symptoms that a general hospital did not have the facilities to cope. Symptoms ranged from hysteria, epilepsy, paralysis, muscle spasms, loss of appetite, inability to speak and many more. There was not a typical number of symptoms; some had many, and others had problems with just one symptom, for example, paralysis.

Some patients were considered insane, as their behaviour was not understood, and they were admitted to hospitals for the mentally insane. St John's Asylum at Bracebridge Heath was one such hospital. Here, patients were considered to be safe; they were locked away from society, often in padded cells, and the hospital at that time used electric shock treatment for a number of conditions and presumed that it would help those patients suffering from shell shock. In actual fact, it frequently made the condition worse and some patients never did leave St John's once they had been admitted.

By 1920, there were to be almost 3,000 dedicated hospital beds for those still suffering with shell shock. The Ministry of Pensions struggled with the concept of shell shock; it was difficult to recognize a disability that did not present itself as an actual physical problem, such as an amputation etc. Physical symptoms may be present, such as severe shaking, muscle cramps, however, once again the problem arose that if the condition did not appear to be directly linked to a specific injury, then how could a disability pension be given? Eventually, the Ministry acknowledged the condition and set about organizing dedicated homes and hospitals where the men could be treated.

At Harrowby Camp Hospital, near Grantham, what had been established as a hospital for taking the wounded during the conflict was to carry on for some years after the end of the Great War. In 1925, the hospital had 230 beds specifically set aside for the treatment of men with shell shock.

The philosophy was simple; occupational therapy was thought to be the way forward, and in order to encourage the men to get back to a full, working life, the men were encouraged to work for six hours a day, doing some occupational chore such as basket weaving, brush making or working on the land. With support, Harrowby Camp Hospital expected that 15 percent of the patients would be able to return to a normal life, and hopefully, receive no further treatment.

In reality, the majority of men suffering with the condition would not be able to return to a normal lifestyle, instead depending on a disability pension to help support them and being treated throughout their lives as outpatients. It has to be remembered that there were many men who suffered from this condition on a minor scale. They may not have sought medical help, but their families would have struggled with mood swings, often violent, debilitating night terrors etc. The official numbers for men with shell shock will never be known because of the stigma attached and the unwillingness of many, and their families, to seek help. It was no bad thing that the Great War had led to women being able to work full time and that they were seen as able to work at a man's job. Many women had to work, simply to support their families and their husband.

The long-term effects of the conflict on the men who fought for our freedom is evident in the following account from a former residential care home worker, now retired.

Almost thirty years ago I worked in a care home in Lincoln and had first-hand experience of knowing a gentleman who had served during World War I and who had suffered from shell shock ever since. So many years had gone by and yet this man still had ongoing problems.

This was a home for elderly residents and wasn't for people who were mentally ill. I was taken round and given a brief introduction to everyone and told a little about them before being given the opportunity to read case notes to familiarize myself with each resident.

This particular gentleman was to be handled with utmost care. On his notes it said that he had suffered from shell shock all his life. Some people might have considered his quirks and foibles as being a result of old age or dementia, but it was obvious that he had been like this since the end of the war.

He couldn't bear to be touched, which was difficult when doing things like shaving etc., and I had to remember to keep one hand behind my back to avoid the temptation to touch his face if I was shaving him. He couldn't keep still and would walk around and around. He could leave the home and would go for walks up and down the street, always the same circuit and doing strange things along the way.

He would talk to you, mumbling an answer without looking you in the eye and if ever anybody dropped anything he was like a rabbit caught in headlights, panicking trying to run away and hide, it was a dreadful thing to see and worse to wonder what kept passing through his mind all those years on. Night times were the worse. Although I didn't do night shifts we would have to read the handover notes, which logged whatever went on during the different shifts. At least twice a week he would have woken, shouting and in great distress and very difficult to comfort someone when touching would distress and even cause violence.

He had no family to visit him as he had never married and apparently lost his only brother during the fighting over there. I don't know whether he was in the Lincoln Regiment, but was certainly originally from Lincoln, so could well have been.

Even now, when I see a programme or documentary on WWI, I always think back to this old chap. With the type of work I used to do I came across other veterans of the war, but none made such a lasting impression as he did. Frightening to think just how many other men, and therefore their families, had to struggle with shell shock and that it could go on for so very long. Thank goodness that the condition has now been recognized and soldiers now serving get the best medical help for Post Traumatic Stress disorder.

Bless them all.

The Great War had ended; too many men had lost their lives, and families across Lincolnshire and the rest of the country would never be the same again. The Great War was now dubbed 'The War to end all Wars', and the country set forth to rebuild the best way it could. Unfortunately, it would only be a relatively few years later that the same families were waving off other family members to fight in another war.

The Lincolnshire Regiment – actions during World War One

(Information taken from Forces War Records
http://www.forces-war-records.co.uk/unit-info/273/)

1st Battalion.

04.08.1914. Stationed at Portsmouth as part of the 9th Brigade of the 3rd Division. (A contingent of the Bermuda Rifle Volunteer Corps of 2 Officers and 125 men also joined the Battalion.)

14.08.1914 Mobilised for war and landed at Havre where the Division engaged in various actions on the Western Front including;

During 1914:
The Battle of Mons and the subsequent retreat, The Battle of Le Cateau, The Battle of the Marne, The Battle of the Aisne, The Battles of La Bassee and Messines, First Battle of Ypres.

During 1915:
Winter Operations 1914-15, The First and Second Attack on Bellewaarde, The Actions of Hooge.
   14.11.1915. Transferred to the 62nd Brigade of the 21st Division and again engaged in various actions on the Western Front including;

During 1916:
The Battle of Albert, The Battle of Bazentin Ridge, The Battle of Flers-Courcelette, The Battle of Morval, The Battle of Le Transloy.

During 1917:
The German retreat to the Hindenburg Line, The First and Third Battles of the Scarpe, The Battle of Polygon Wood, The Battle of Broodseinde, The Second Battle of Passchendaele, The Cambrai Operations.

During 1918:
The Battle of St Quentin, The First Battle of Bapaume, The Battle of Messines, The Second Battle of Kemmel, The Battle of the Aisne 1918, The Battle of Albert, The Second Battle of Bapaume, The Battle of Epehy, The Battle of the St Quentin Canal, The Battle of Cambrai 1918, The Battle of the Selle.

11.11.1918 Ended the war in France, Aymeries north of Aulnoye.

2nd Battalion.

04.08.1914 Stationed in Bermuda at the outbreak of war and then moved to Halifax, Nova Scotia.

03.10.1914 Embarked for the UK landing at Devonport, Plymouth and then moved to Hursley Park, Winchester, to join the 25th Brigade of the 8th Division.

06.11.1914 Mobilised for war and landed at Havre where the Division engaged in various actions on the Western Front including;

During 1915:
The Battle of Neuve Chapelle, The Battle of Aubers, The action of Bois Grenier.

During 1916:
The Battle of Albert.

During 1917:
The German retreat to the Hindenburg Line, The Battle of Pilkem, The Battle of Langemarck.

04.02.1918 Transferred to the 62nd Brigade of the 21st Division.

During 1918:
The Battle of St Quentin, The First and Second Battle of Bapaume, The Battle of Messines, The Second Battle of Kemmel, The Battle of the Aisne 1918, The Battle of Albert, The Battle of Epehy, The Battle of the St Quentin Canal, The Battle of Cambrai 1918, The Battle of the Selle.

11.11.1918 Ended the war in France, Aymeries north of Aulnoye.

3rd Battalion.

04.08.1918 Stationed at Lincoln then moved to Grimsby and then Cork, Ireland in 1918.

1/4th Battalion, Territorial Force.

04.08.1914 Stationed at Lincoln as part of the Lincoln & Leicester Brigade of the North Midland Division.

11.08.1914 Moved to Belper and then Luton.

01.03.1915 Mobilised for war and landed at Havre. The formation became the 138th Brigade of the 46th Division which engaged in various actions on the Western Front including;

The German liquid fire attack at Hooge, The attack at the Hohenzollern Redoubt.

07.01.1916 Embarked Alexandria from Marseilles.

04.02.1916 Embarked for France from Alexandria, landing in Marseilles 09.02.1916. The Division once again engaged in actions on the Western Front including;

During 1916:

The diversionary attack at Gommecourt.

During 1917:

Operations on the Ancre, occupation of the Gommecourt defences, the attack on Rettemoy Graben, The German retreat to the Hindenburg Line, The attack on Lievin, The Battle of Hill 70.

31.01.1918 Transferred to the 177th Brigade of the 59th Division, absorbing 2/4th Battalion and engaged in various actions including; The Battle of Bapaume, The Battle of Bailleul, The First Battle of Kemmel Ridge.

08.05.1918 Reduced to training cadre and transferred to the 49th Brigade of the 16th Division.

17.06.1918 Transferred to the 102nd Brigade of the 34th Division.

27.06.1918 Transferred first to the 117th and then the 116th Brigade of the 39th Division.

1/5th Battalion, Territorial Force.

04.08.1918 Stationed at Grimsby as part of the Lincoln & Leicester Brigade of the North Midland Division.

11.08.1914 Moved to Belper and then Luton.

01.03.1915 Mobilised for war and landed at Havre. The formation became the 138th Brigade of the 46th Division which engaged in various actions on the Western Front including;

The German liquid fire attack at Hooge, The attack at the Hohenzollern Redoubt.

07.01.1916 Embarked Alexandria from Marseilles.

04.02.1916 Embarked for France from Alexandria landing in Marseilles 09.02.1916. The Division once again engaged in actions on the Western Front including;

During 1916:

The diversionary attack at Gommecourt.

During 1917:

Operations on the Ancre, occupation of the Gommecourt defences, The attack on Rettemoy Graben, The German retreat to the Hindenburg Line, The attack on Lievin, The Battle of Hill 70.

During 1918:

The Battle of the St Quentin Canal, The Battle of the Beaurevoir Line, The Battle of Cambrai, The Battle of the Selle, The Battle of Sambre.

11.11.1918 Ended the war in France, Sains du Nord S.E. of Avesnes.

2/4th Battalion, Territorial Force.

13.09.1914 Formed in Lincoln and then moved to St. Albans to join the 177th Brigade of the 59th Division.

April 1916 Moved to Dublin and Fermoy, Ireland.

Jan 1917 Returned to England at Fovant, Wiltshire.

Feb 1917 Mobilised for war and landed in France, where the Division engaged in various actions on the Western Front including;

The pursuit of the German retreat to the Hindenburg Line, The Battle of the Menin Road Ridge, The Battle of Polygon Wood, The capture of Bourlon Wood.

31.01.1918 Absorbed by the 1/4th Battalion.

2/5th Battalion, Territorial Force.

06.02.1915 Formed at Grimsby and then moved to St. Albans to join the 177th Brigade of the 59th Division.

April 1916 Moved to Dublin and Fermoy, Ireland.

Jan 1917 Returned to England at Fovant, Wiltshire.

Feb 1917 Mobilised for war and landed in France, where the Division engaged in various actions on the Western Front including;

The pursuit of the German retreat to the Hindenburg Line, The Battle of the Menin Road Ridge, The Battle of Polygon Wood, The capture of Bourlon Wood.

08.05.1918 Reduced to training cadre, then transferred to the 21st Brigade of the 30th Division.

31.07.1918 Absorbed by the 1/5th Battalion.

3/4th and 3/5th Battalions, Territorial Force.

01.06.1915 & 17.04.1915 Formed at Lincoln and Grimsby.

08.04.1916 Became the 4th and 5th Reserve Battalions at Grantham.

01.09.1916 The 4th absorbed the 5th as part of the North Midland Reserve Brigade.

6th (Service) Battalion.

Aug 1914 Formed at Lincoln as part of the First New Army (K1) and then moved to Belton Park, Grantham as part of the 33rd Brigade of the 11th Division.

April 1915 Moved to Frensham.

01.07.1915 Mobilised for war and embarked for Gallipoli from Liverpool via Alexandria and Mudros.

20-30.07.1915 At Cape Helles.

07.08.1915 Landed at Suvla Bay and the Division engaged in various actions including; The Battle of Scimitar Hill and attack on Hill 60.

21.12.1915 Evacuated from Gallipoli due to heavy losses from combat, disease and severe weather.

02.02.1916 Moved to Alexandria to take over defences of the Suez Canal.

02.07.1916 Embarked for France from Alexandria, landing at Marseilles by 08.07.1916 and the Division engaged in various actions on the Western Front including;

The capture of the Wundt-Werk, The Battle of Flers-Courcelette, The Battle of Thiepval,

During 1917:

Operations on the Ancre, The Battle of Messines, The Battle of the

Langemarck, The Battle of Polygon Wood, The Battle of Broodseinde, The Battle of Poelcapelle.

During 1918:
The Battle of the Scarpe, The Battle of the Drocourt-Quant Line, The Battle of the Canal du Nord, The Battle of Cambrai 1918, The pursuit to the Selle, The Battle of the Sambre.

11.11.1918 Ended the war in Belgium near Aulnois north of Maubeuge.

7th (Service) Battalion.

Sept 1914 Formed at Lincoln as part of the Second New Army (K2) and then moved to Wool as part of the 51st Brigade of the 17th Division.

June 1915 Moved to Winchester.

14.07.1915 Mobilised for war, landed at Boulogne, and the Division engaged in various actions on the Western Front including;

During 1916:
Actions of Spring 1916, The Battle of Albert, The Battle of Delville Wood.

During 1917:
The First and Second Battles of the Scarpe, The Capture of Roeux, The First and Second Battles of Passchendaele.

During 1918:
The Battle of St Quentin, The Battle of Bapaume, The Battle of Amiens, The Battle of Albert, The Battle of Bapaume, The Battle of Havrincourt, The Battle of Epehy, The Battle of Cambrai 1918, The pursuit to the Selle, The Battle of the Selle, The Battle of the Sambre.

11.11.1918 Ended the war in France, Aulnoye south of Maubeuge.

8th (Service) Battalion.

Sept 1914 Formed at Lincoln as part of the Third New Army (K3) and then moved to Halton Park, Tring, as part of the 21st Brigade of the 21st Division, and then moved to Leighton Buzzard.

April 1915 Moved back to Halton Park and then Witley.

10.09.1915 Mobilised for war, landed at Boulogne, and the Division engaged in various actions on the Western Front including;

During 1915:
The Battle of Loos.

08.07.1916 Transferred to the 63rd Brigade of the 37th Division and continued to engaged in various actions on the Western Front including;

During 1916:

The Battle of the Ancre.

During 1917:

The First and Second Battles of the Scarpe, The Battle of Arleux, The Battle of Pilkem Ridge, The Battle of the Menin Road Ridge, The Battle of Polygon Wood, The Battle of Broodseinde, The Battle of Poelcapelle, The First Battle of Passchendaele.

During 1918:

The Battle of the Ancre, The Battle of the Albert, The Battle of Havrincourt, The Battle of the Canal du Nord, The Battle of Cambrai, The pursuit to the Selle, The Battle of the Selle, The Battle of the Sambre.

11.11.1918 Ended the war in France, Neuville S.W. of Le Quesnoy.

9th (Service) Battalion.

Nov 1914 Formed at Lincoln as a Service battalion of the Fourth New Army (K4) in the 91st Brigade of the 30th Division.

10.04.1915   Formation became the 2nd Reserve Battalion of the 3rd Reserve Brigade and moved to Lichfield and then Brocton.

01.09.1916 Became the 11th Training Reserve Battalion.

10th (Service) Battalion (Grimsby).

09.09.1914 Formed by the Mayor and Town of Grimsby, and then moved to Brocklesby.

June 1915 Moved to Ripon to join the 101st Brigade of the 34th Division.

10.08.1915 Taken over by the War Office and moved to Perham Down and then Sutton Veny.

09.01.1916 Mobilised for war and landed in France, and the Division engaged in various actions n the Western Front including;

During 1916:

The Battle of Albert, The Battle of Bazentin Ridge, The Battle of Pozieres Ridge.

During 1917:

The First and Second Battles of the Scarpe, The Battle of Arleux, The fighting at Hargicourt, The Third Battles of Ypres.

03.02.1918 Transferred to the 103rd Brigade of the same Division and continued to engage in various actions including;

During 1918:

The Battle of St Quentin, The Battle of Estaires, The Battle of Bailleul, The First Battle for Kemmel Ridge.

18.05.1918 Reduced to training cadre.

17.06.1918 Transferred to the 116th Brigade of the 39th Division.

16.08.1918 Transferred to the 66th Division.

20.09.1918 Transferred to the 197th Brigade to defend the lines of communication near Aumle.

11th (Reserve) Battalion.

Oct 1915 Formed from the depot companies of the 10th Battalion at Lincoln as a Reserve Battalion.

Jan 1916 Moved to Harrogate to join the 19th Reserve Brigade and then moved to Durham.

01.09.1916 Became the 82nd training Reserve Battalion of the 19th Reserve Brigade at Newcastle.

12th (Labour) Battalion.

July 1916 Formed at Brocklesby.

Aug 1916 Moved to France to work on the Lines of Communication.

April 1917 Transferred to the Labour Corps as the 16th and 17th Labour Corps.

13th Battalion, Territorial Force.

01.01.1917 Formed in Bath from the 28th Provisional Battalion as part of the 215th Brigade of the 72nd Division then moved to Bedford.

May 1917 Moved to Ipswich

31.10.1917 Disbanded.

1st Garrison Battalion.

Sept 1915 Formed and went to India by Oct.

2nd (Home Service) Garrison Battalion.

May 1916 Formed at North Coates, Grimsby.

Aug 1917 Became the 4th Battalion Royal Defence Corps.

Index

4th Northern General Hospital, 32–3, 35, 75, 79

Admiralty Landships Committee, 27–8
Advanced Dressing Station, 3
Aircraft Production, 49–53
 Clayton & Shuttleworth, 50–1
 Marshall, Sons & Co, 52–3
 Ruston, Proctor & Co, 51–2
Airship, 20, 22
 Sleaford crash, 22
 Army Remount Service, 46–9
Avro 504, 20

Base Hospital, 34
Battle of Mons, 35
Battle of the Somme, 15
Bennet, George, 14
BE2c, 20
Big Willie, 30
Boultham Park Hall, 35
Brocklesby Hall, 35

Caistor, 14
Carrier Pigeons, 23–4
Conscription, 18

Disability, 16
Drill Hall, Lincoln, 34

Flers, 30

Food production, 53, 56

Gas, 16
George V, King, 73–6
Grantham, 18
Grimsby, 14
Grimsby Chums, The, 13–18
 Earl of Yarborough, 14
 La Boiselle, 15

Heanage, George, 14

Influenza Epidemic, 78–81
Immingham, 14

Kirman, Pte Charles, 82–3
Kitchener, Lord, 13

Labour Corps, 56–8
Laceby, 14
Lewis, Pte Sidney, 18
Lincoln City Football Club, 24, 78
Lincoln Grammar School, 32
Lincoln War Memorial, 80
Lincolnshire Poacher Song, the, 39
Lincolnshire Regiment, 12, 14, 37–43, 87–95
 Earl of Bath's Regiment of Foot, 37
 Sobraon Barracks, 3-8
 The Poachers, 38
Little Willie, 29

Observation Kite Balloons, 20-1

Point du Jour, Vimy Ridge, 17
    10th Battalion Grimsby Chums,
        17
Prisoners of War, 59–63

Rationing, 76–7
Recruitment, 12
Red Cross, 35
RFC Anwick Landing Ground, 21
    38 Squadron, 21
Rigby, William, 28
Royal Naval Air Service, Cranwell,
    19
    Paine, Cdre Godfrey M., 19

Shell Shock, 83–6
Shepherd, Matron, 35
Smith, Edith, 43–4
    Womens' Police Volunteers, 44
Somme, the, 19
St Dunstan's, 16
Swinton, Lt Col Ernest, 27

Tank, 29
Tank Bank, 70–2

Victoria Cross, 40–2
    Clarke, Acting Cpl Charles
        Richard, 41
    Evans, Sgt Arthur, 41
    Hansen, Capt Percy Howard, 41
Voluntary Aid Detachment, 35

Warrener, Sgt John William, 67–8
Wilson, Walter, 28, 30
War Memorials, 81
Widow's Pension, 16
William Foster & Co, 27–8
White feathers, 19
White Hart Hotel, Lincoln, 28
Wintringham Grammar School, 15
Women's Land Army, 69

Yellowbellies, 37

Zeppelin, 21, 30–1, 45–6, 69–70